Higher Education in Developing Countries

Peril and Promise

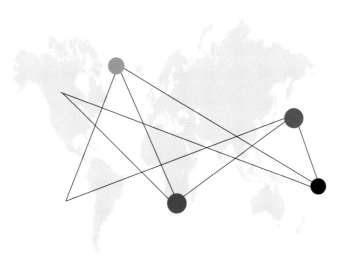

THE TASK FORCE ON HIGHER EDUCATION AND SOCIETY

©2000 The International Bank for Reconstruction and
Development / THE WORLD BANK
1818 H Street, N.W.
Washington, D.C. 20433, U.S.A.

Book design by Naylor Design, Inc.

ISBN: 0-8213-4630-X

Library of Congress Cataloging-in-Publication Data is in process

Published for the Task Force on Higher Education and Society
by the World Bank

1818 H Street, NW
Washington, DC 20433, USA
Telephone: 202-477-1234
Facsimile: 202-477-6391
Telex: MCI 64145WORLDBANK
         MCI 248423WORLDBANK
World Wide Web: http://www.worldbank.org
E-mail: books@worldbank.org

Contents

Boxes, Figures, and Tables

Boxes

Figures

Tables

Statistical Appendix Tables

Acknowledgments

The Task Force on Higher Education in Developing Countries was convened by the World Bank and The United Nations Educational, Scientific and Cultural Organization (UNESCO).

Task Force Members

Mamphela Ramphele	(South Africa) Vice-Chancellor, University of Cape Town (Co-chair and Steering Committee)
Henry Rosovsky	(United States) Former Dean of the Faculty of Arts & Sciences and Geyser University Professor Emeritus, Harvard University (Co-chair and Steering Committee)
Kenneth Prewitt	(United States) Director, US Bureau of the Census (Vice-chair and Steering Committee)
Babar Ali	(Pakistan) Pro-Chancellor, Lahore University of Management Sciences
Hanan Ashrawi	(Palestine) Former Minister for Higher Education
José Joaquín Brunner	(Chile) Director, Education Program, Fundación Chile and former Minister Secretary General
Lone Dybkjær	(Denmark) Member, European Parliament and former Minister for the Environment
José Goldemberg	(Brazil) Professor, University of São Paulo and former Minister of Education
Georges Haddad	(France) Professor, University of Paris/ Panthéon-Sorbonne
Motoo Kaji	(Japan) Vice-President, University of the Air
Jajah Koswara	(Indonesia) Director, Research and Community Service Development, Directorate General of Higher Education
Narciso Matos	(Mozambique) Secretary-General, Association of African Universities
Manmohan Singh	(India) Member of Parliament and former Minister of Finance
Carl Tham	(Sweden) Secretary General, Olof Palme International Center and former Minister of Education and Science

Study Co-Directors

Kamal Ahmad   (United States) Attorney, Fried, Frank, Harris, Shriver & Jacobson
(Steering Committee)

David E. Bloom   (United States) Professor, Harvard University
(Steering Committee and Head of Task Force Secretariat)

Not all members of the Task Force attended every meeting or commented on every draft. Individual differences concerning specific points may remain, but the document represents the consensus of all Task Force members. The principal drafters of this report were David Bloom and Henry Rosovsky.

Task Force Supporters

In preparing this report, the Task Force was greatly assisted by numerous individuals, whose support we would particularly like to acknowledge.

Those who made substantive contributions, either verbally or in writing:

Berhanu Abegaz; Dennis Aigner; Gregory Armstrong; Michael Aronson; Roberto Arruda; Saleem Badat; Jorge Balán; Charles Beirne; David Bell; Lakshmi Reddy Bloom; Derek Bok; Carolina Bori; Lewis Branscombe; Harvey Brooks; David Canning; Hernán Chaimovich; Richard Chait; Muhamed Ibn Chambas; The Civic Education Project; Joel Cohen; David Court; Veena Das; Satish Dhavan; Ronald Dore; Eunice Durham; Eva Egron-Polak; Donald Ekong; Ahmed Essop; William Experton; Anna Maria Fanelli; Brian Figaji; Malcolm Gillis; Merle Goldman; Xabier Gorostiaga, SJ; Ada Pellegrini Grinover; Göran Grosskopf; Wadi Haddad; Emily Hannum; Chester Haskell; Ruth Hayhoe; Robert Herdt; Werner Hirsch; Lauritz Holm-Nielsen; Gerald Holton; Adam Jaffe; Dimandja Kasongo; Shamsh Kassim-Lakha; Tom Kessinger; Riaz Khan; Miryam Krasilchik; Suzanne Grant Lewis; Gustavo López Ospina; William Loxley; Jacob Mamabolo; Jacques Markovich; Noel McGinn; G. A. Miana; Daniel Morales-Gomez; José Ignacio Moreno León; Claudio de Moura Castro; Sarah Newberry; Dorothy Njeuma; Berit Olsson; Maris O'Rourke; Solomea Pavlychko; Vicky Phillips; Pasuk Phongpaichit; Luis Piazzón; Colin Power; Sivraj Ramaseshan; Amulya Reddy; Francisco Rivera-Batiz; Jeffrey Sachs; Sarah Sievers; Jan Sadlak; William Saint; Jamil Salmi; Komlavi F. Seddoh; Patrick Seyon; Khalid Hamid Sheikh; Jim Shute; Zillur Rahman Siddiqui; Andrew Sillen; S. Frederick Starr; Rolf Stumpf; Simon Schwartzman; Jamsheer Talati; Lewis Tyler; Emily Vargas-Baron; Hebe Vessuri; Louis Wells; Francis Wilson; Nan Yeld; and Harriet Zuckerman.

The Task Force also wishes to warmly recognize the generous financial support it received from the following organizations:

The Canadian International Development Agency
The Ford Foundation
The Norwegian Agency for Development Cooperation
The Novartis Foundation for Sustainable Development
The Rockefeller Foundation
The Swedish International Development Agency
The Tetra Laval Group
The William and Flora Hewlett Foundation
The World Bank

The support of one donor, who wishes to remain anonymous, is also gratefully acknowledged.

Special Thanks

The Task Force would particularly like to thank the following for their outstanding efforts on its behalf:

Ismail Serageldin, who (along with Kamal Ahmad) recognized early on the need for an independent examination of higher education in the context of international development and whose efforts resulted in the establishment and initial funding of the Task Force; Joan Martin-Brown, who also provided enormously practical encouragement and assistance in these efforts; Larry Rosenberg, whose substantive and administrative contributions to every aspect of the Task Force were truly exceptional; Philip Altbach, who served as a special consultant to the Steering Committee of the Task Force and whose extensive comments and suggestions are reflected throughout this report; Ava Cheloff, who performed the Herculean task of organizing the statistical appendix; Ruth Kagia, who did a magnificent job moving the Task Force report from manuscript to publication; and River Path Associates, which did an extraordinary job of editing the manuscript and aiding the Task Force in expressing its ideas as clearly and cogently as possible.

In-Kind Contributions

Several important in-kind contributions facilitated the work of the Task Force, which would like to express its gratitude to:

The Aga Khan Development Network
The Aga Khan University
The Harvard Institute for International Development
The Harvard School of Public Health
The law firm of Fried, Frank, Harris, Shriver & Jacobson
The Social Science Research Council
UNESCO
The University of Cape Town
The University of São Paulo
The World Bank

Research Assistants

The following individuals, who are warmly thanked by the Task Force, provided outstanding research assistance to the Task Force Secretariat:

Xiaonan Cao; Bryan Graham; Amar Hamoudi; Richard Hopper; Erin Kleindorfer; Stefanie Koch; Andrew Mellinger; Atif Rizvi; and Carolyn Wood.

Administrative Support

Strong administrative support was crucial to the work of the Task Force, which would like to register its appreciation to:

Ida Cooper; Rula Dajani; Jeanne Damlamian; Alice Dowsett; Anders Falk; Laura Fusaro; Helen Goodman; Sarwat Hussain; Vivian Jackson; Amina Jacobs; Nancy Juskin; Gail Kovach; Brett Kravitz; Ellen Lee; Sarah Newberry; Maria Papadopoulos; Enid Sinequan; and Vera Helena Vieira.

Seminar Participants

Helpful comments on earlier versions of this report were received from participants in seminars and symposia conducted at:

The Aga Khan University
The Goddard Space Flight Center
Harvard University Graduate School of Education
National Academy of Sciences and Humanities, Jerusalem
The National University of Singapore
UNESCO General Conference

Seminar Hosts

Further thanks go to the gracious hosts of the various meetings of the Task Force:

The World Bank (Washington, D.C., United States, October 1997)
The University of Cape Town (Cape Town, South Africa, February 1998)
The Aga Khan Development Network (Geneva, Switzerland, September 1998)
The University of São Paulo (São Paulo, Brazil, January 1999)
The Social Science Research Council (New York, United States, July 1999)

And finally…

There are always a large number of other people and organizations who provide, in different ways, support, encouragement, and ideas during such a far-reaching and ambitious project. It is, of course, impossible to thank them all by name, but their help is much appreciated.

The Task Force website is www.tfhe.net, where electronic copies of the report can be searched and downloaded. The Task Force can be contacted at info@tfhe.net.

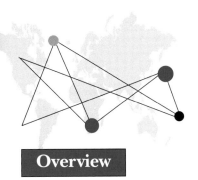

Human history becomes more and more a race between education and catastrophe.

H.G. Wells, *The Outline of History*

The Task Force

The Task Force on Higher Education and Society was convened by the World Bank and UNESCO to bring together experts from 13 countries for the purpose of exploring the future of higher education in the developing world.

Based on research and intensive discussion and hearings conducted over a two-year period, the Task Force has concluded that, without more and better higher education, developing countries will find it increasingly difficult to benefit from the global knowledge-based economy.

The Task Force has attempted to clarify the arguments for higher education development, especially from the standpoint of public policymakers and the international community. It has also diagnosed specific problems that are common across the developing world—home to more than 80 percent of the world's population—and suggested potential solutions. *Higher Education in Developing Countries: Peril and Promise* is split into six chapters, which address:

- higher education's long-standing problems and the new realities it faces;

- the nature of the public interest in higher education;

- the issue of how focusing on higher education as a system will yield the benefits of planned diversification;

- the need to improve standards of governance;

- the particularly acute requirement for better science and technology education; and

- a call to develop imaginative general education curricula for certain students.

Peril and Promise

The world economy is changing as knowledge supplants physical capital as the source of present (and future) wealth. Technology is driving much of this process, with information technology, biotechnology, and other innovations leading to remarkable changes in the way we live and work.

As knowledge becomes more important, so does higher education. Countries need to educate more of their young people to a higher standard—a degree is now a basic qualification for many skilled jobs. The quality of knowledge generated within higher education institutions, and its availability to the wider economy, is becoming increasingly critical to national competitiveness.

This poses a serious challenge to the developing world. Since the 1980s, many national governments and international donors have assigned higher education a relatively low priority. Narrow—and, in our view, misleading—economic analysis has contributed to the view that public investment in universities and colleges brings meager returns compared to investment in primary and secondary schools, and that higher education magnifies income inequality.

As a result, higher education systems in developing countries are under great strain. They are chronically underfunded, but face escalating demand—approximately half of today's higher education students live in the developing world. Faculty are often underqualified, lack motivation, and are poorly rewarded. Students are poorly taught and curricula underdeveloped. Developed countries, meanwhile, are constantly raising the stakes. Quite simply, many developing countries will need to work much harder just to maintain their position, let alone catch up. There are notable exceptions, but currently, across most of the developing world, the potential of higher education to promote development is being realized only marginally.

Wider Focus

The Task Force is united in the belief that urgent action to expand the quantity and improve the quality of higher education in developing countries should be a top development priority. Developing countries need higher education to:

- provide increasing numbers of students, especially those from disadvantaged backgrounds, with specialized skills, because specialists are increasingly in demand in all sectors of the world economy;

- produce a body of students with a general education that encourages flexibility and innovation, thus allowing the continual renewal of economic and social structures relevant to a fast-changing world;

- teach students not just what is currently known, but also how to keep their knowledge up to date, so that they will be able to refresh their skills as the economic environment changes; and

- increase the amount and quality of in-country research, thus allowing the developing world to select, absorb, and create new knowledge more efficiently and rapidly than it currently does.

The Task Force recognizes that there are many difficulties in achieving these aims, including the plethora of competing demands for public money. Action, therefore, will need creativity and persistence. A new vision of what higher education can achieve is required, combined with better planning and higher standards of management. The strengths of all players—public and private—must be used, with the international community at last emerging to provide strong and coordinated support and leadership in this critical area.

System Focus

The Task Force recommends that each developing country make it a national priority to debate and determine what it can realistically expect its higher education system to deliver. The debate must be informed by historical and comparative knowledge about the contribution of higher education to social, economic, and political development—but also should take clear account of the challenges the future will bring. It should establish for each higher education system clear goals that policymakers can use to view the higher education system as a whole, determining what each part can contribute to the public good.

This kind of holistic analysis of higher education systems has rarely been attempted. It does not mean reverting to centrally planned systems—far from it. Instead, it offers the ability to balance strategic direction with the diversity now found in higher education systems across the developing world. This diversification—a reaction to increased demand—has brought new providers (especially from the private sector) into the system and encouraged new types of institutions to emerge. It promises increased competition and, ultimately, improved quality.

Unfortunately, this promise will not be delivered if diversification continues to be chaotic and unplanned. Players, new and old, will thrive only in higher education systems that develop core qualities. These qualities include:

- sufficient autonomy, with governments providing clear supervision, while avoiding day-to-day management;

- explicit stratification, allowing institutions to play to their strengths and serve different needs, while competing for funding, faculty, and students;

- cooperation as well as competition, whereby human and physical capital, as well as knowledge and ideas, can be profitably shared within the system, creating, for example, a "learning commons" where facilities—computers, libraries, and laboratories—are open to all students; and

- increased openness, encouraging higher education institutions to develop knowledge- (and revenue-) sharing links with business and to deepen the dialogue with society that will lead to stronger democracy and more resilient nation states.

On its own, the market will certainly not devise this kind of system. Markets require profit and this can crowd out important educational duties and opportunities. Basic sciences and the humanities, for example, are essential for national development. They are likely to be underfunded, unless they are actively encouraged by leaders in education who have the resources to realize this vision.

Governments need to develop a new role as supervisors, rather than directors, of higher education. They should concentrate on establishing the parameters within which success can be achieved, while allowing specific solutions to emerge from the creativity of higher education professionals.

Practical Solutions

The Task Force has identified a number of areas where immediate, practical action is needed. These include:

- **funding**—the Task Force suggests a mixed funding model to maximize the financial input of the private sector, philanthropic individuals and institutions, and students. It also calls for more consistent and productive public funding mechanisms.

- **resources**—the Task Force makes practical suggestions for the more effective use of physical and human capital, including an urgent plea for access to the new technologies needed to connect developing countries to the global intellectual mainstream.

- **governance**—the Task Force proposes a set of principles of good governance (acknowledged by many as the central problem facing higher education in developing countries) and discusses tools that promote their implementation; better management will lead to the more effective deployment of limited resources.

Figure 1

Tertiary Enrollment Ratios, 1995

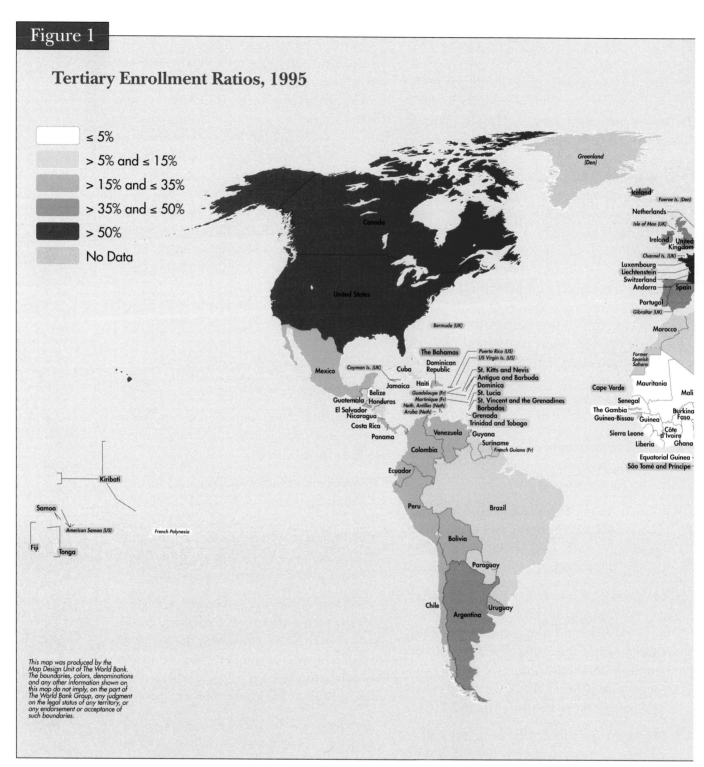

Legend:
- ≤ 5%
- > 5% and ≤ 15%
- > 15% and ≤ 35%
- > 35% and ≤ 50%
- > 50%
- No Data

This map was produced by the Map Design Unit of The World Bank. The boundaries, colors, denominations and any other information shown on this map do not imply, on the part of The World Bank Group, any judgment on the legal status of any territory, or any endorsement or acceptance of such boundaries.

This map shows the variation in tertiary gross enrollment ratios across the countries of the world. In general, people in countries that are more developed economically are more likely to be enrolled in higher education. Nevertheless, there are also regional trends, and numerous countries have different enrollment ratios than might be expected on the basis of per-capita income.

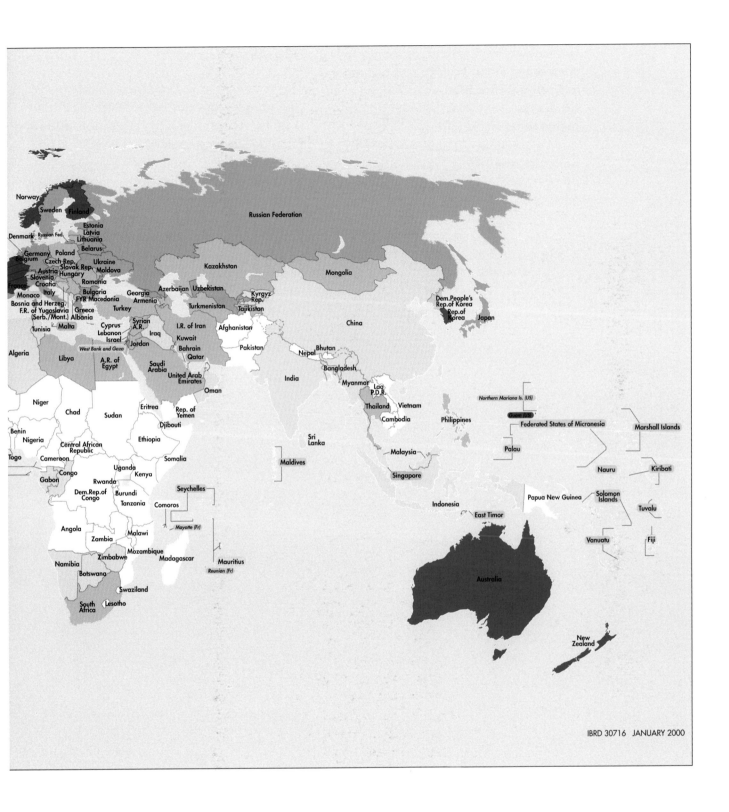

Norway
Sweden
Finland
Denmark
Russian Fed.
Estonia
Latvia
Lithuania
Belarus
Germany Poland
Belgium
Czech Rep.
Austria Slovak Rep.
Slovenia Hungary
France Croatia
Monaco Italy Romania
Bosnia and Herzeg. Bulgaria
F.R. of Yugoslavia FYR Macedonia
(Serb./Mont.) Albania
Tunisia Malta
Cyprus
Syrian
A.R.
Lebanon
Israel
Jordan
West Bank and Gaza
Algeria
Libya
A.R. of
Egypt
Georgia
Armenia
Azerbaijan Uzbekistan
Turkmenistan
Kyrgyz
Rep.
Tajikistan
I.R. of Iran
Afghanistan
Kuwait
Bahrain
Qatar
Saudi
Arabia
United Arab
Emirates
Oman
Russian Federation
Kazakhstan
Mongolia
China
Dem.People's
Rep.of Korea
Rep.of
Korea
Japan
Pakistan
Nepal
Bhutan
Bangladesh
India
Myanmar
Lao
P.D.R.
Thailand
Vietnam
Cambodia
Philippines
Sri
Lanka
Maldives
Malaysia
Singapore
Northern Mariana Is. (US)
Guam (US)
Federated States of Micronesia
Palau
Marshall Islands
Nauru
Kiribati
Indonesia
East Timor
Papua New Guinea
Solomon
Islands
Tuvalu
Vanuatu
Fiji
Niger
Chad
Sudan
Eritrea
Rep. of
Yemen
Djibouti
Benin
Nigeria
Central African
Republic
Ethiopia
Somalia
Togo
Cameroon
Congo
Gabon
Uganda
Kenya
Rwanda
Dem.Rep.of
Congo
Burundi
Tanzania
Seychelles
Comoros
Mayotte (Fr)
Angola
Malawi
Zambia
Mozambique
Zimbabwe
Madagascar
Mauritius
Reunion (Fr)
Namibia
Botswana
Swaziland
South
Africa
Lesotho
Australia
New
Zealand

IBRD 30716 JANUARY 2000

- **curriculum development, especially in two contrasting areas, science and technology, and general education**—the Task Force believes that, in the knowledge economy, highly trained specialists and broadly educated generalists will be at a premium, and both will need to be educated more flexibly so that they continue to learn as their environment develops.

The Way Forward

Higher Education in Developing Countries: Peril and Promise does not offer a universal blueprint for reforming higher education systems, but it does provide a starting point for action. The greatest desire of the Task Force is to catalyze dialogue in countries around the world. While the benefits of higher education continue to rise, the costs of being left behind are also growing. Higher education is no longer a luxury: it is essential to national social and economic development.

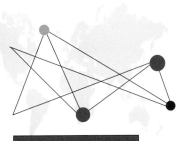

Introduction

Today, more than ever before in human history, the wealth—or poverty—of nations depends on the quality of higher education. Those with a larger repertoire of skills and a greater capacity for learning can look forward to lifetimes of unprecedented economic fulfillment. But in the coming decades the poorly educated face little better than the dreary prospects of lives of quiet desperation.

Malcolm Gillis, President of Rice University, 12 February 1999

Today, global wealth is concentrated less and less in factories, land, tools, and machinery. The knowledge, skills, and resourcefulness of people are increasingly critical to the world economy. Human capital in the United States is now estimated to be at least three times more important than physical capital. A century ago, this would not have been the case.

The developed world is reacting quickly, with education a major political priority. High-quality human capital is developed in high-quality education systems, with tertiary education providing the advanced skills that command a premium in today's workplace. Most developed countries have seen a substantial rise in the proportion of their young people receiving higher education. Lifelong learning is also being used to help workers adjust to rapidly changing economies.

And what about developing countries?[1] Will they be able to compete in the knowledge economy or do they face a future of increasing exclusion, unable to develop the skills required for the twenty-first century? This challenge is well understood by most residents of the developing world. President Benjamin W. Mkapa of Tanzania, for example, is concerned that higher education in Africa is becoming increasingly obsolete. "Our universities," he says, "must produce men and women willing to fight an intellectual battle for self-confidence and self-assertion as equal players in the emerging globalized world."

In light of these concerns, this report asks the following three questions:

- What is the role of higher education in supporting and enhancing the process of economic and social development?

- What are the major obstacles that higher education faces in developing countries?

- How can these obstacles best be overcome?

Some readers will be surprised that we spend this time reiterating arguments for the importance of higher education. After all, educa-

---

[1] "Developing country" is not a precise term, although more than 80 percent of the world's population lives in a developing country, as conventionally defined by the World Bank on the basis of income per capita. Our overview includes Africa, much of Asia, nearly all of Latin America, and large parts of the former Soviet Union. Clearly, the developing world exhibits tremendous variation culturally, politically, socially, and economically. However, we are confident that general principles exist and have focused on issues that arise most frequently, drawing conclusions that can be applied in many different countries. Exceptions do exist of course, and some readers will feel that certain points do not apply in their country. We hope this reaction will be rare.

tion is associated with better skills, higher productivity, and enhanced human capacity to improve the quality of life. Education at all levels is needed if economies are to climb from subsistence farming, through an economy based on manufacturing, to participation in the global knowledge economy.

During the past two or three decades, however, attention has focused on primary education, especially for girls. This has led to a neglect of secondary and tertiary education, with higher education in a perilous state in many, if not most, developing countries. With a few notable exceptions, it is underfunded by governments and donors. As a result, quality is low and often deteriorating, while access remains limited. Higher education institutions (and whole systems) are politicized, poorly regulated, and sometimes corrupt.

We believe that a more balanced approach to education at all levels is needed. The focus on primary education is important, but an approach that pursues primary education alone will leave societies dangerously unprepared for survival in tomorrow's world.

New Realities

Within a few decades of the end of World War II, the major colonial empires had disintegrated. Initially, newly independent countries, and poorer countries more generally, looked to their higher education systems to deliver support for national efforts to raise standards of living and alleviate poverty. They also attempted to widen access to higher education and, in some cases, there was a belief that higher education could help make societies more democratic, while strengthening human rights.

No country can claim complete success in achieving these traditional "nation-building" goals, but in most countries some progress has been made on all three fronts. Since the 1960s,

higher education has been forced to confront what we refer to as the "new realities": *expansion, differentiation,* and the *knowledge revolution.* These are changing higher education and the environment in which it exists. All are now powerful influences in developing countries, challenging policymakers to look afresh at their systems of higher education and think creatively about what they can achieve.

Expansion is a result of the tremendous increase in the number of students. In the 1940s and 1950s, higher education in developing countries was characterized by few students and graduates, with the students frequently in training for either the (colonial) civil service or a few professions. Today, however, there has been a dramatic shift from class to mass, with half of the world's students of higher education living in developing countries. As more and more children complete their primary and secondary education, many wish to continue to gain a degree. Developing countries have also seen real incomes rising, bringing further education within the reach of an increasing number of families.

Expansion has produced a variety of consequences. In many instances, existing institutions have grown in size, transforming themselves into mega-universities; in other cases, traditional institutions have been replicated by public or private means. An even more creative response has been seen in *differentiation,* a process whereby new types of institutions are born and new providers enter the sector. Developing countries now have a tremendous variety of colleges and universities, instead of the small number of homogeneous institutions existing 50 years ago. Private institutions have joined public ones,[2] while a range of

---

[2] The terms "public" and "private" are frequently used in this report to describe institutions of higher education. "Private," in particular, requires cautious application. Some private schools are philanthropic entities and are not for profit. Generating surpluses is not the dominant motive of these organizations, and in that sense they resemble state schools.

vocational and professional schools now complement the traditional universities.

Expansion has caused the average quality of education to decline in many countries as resources are stretched increasingly thin. Developing countries now need to clarify the national benefit they receive from education systems and to explore the results that a differentiated (and usually unplanned) system delivers. Private institutions are currently growing most quickly, and there is an especially urgent need to explore what the private sector can and cannot deliver. Policymakers can then plan for the orderly development of a higher education system; establish mechanisms to maintain quality; and, most importantly, nurture areas for which private funds are unlikely to be available. These include basic scientific research, support for the humanities, and scholarship support to increase access for underrepresented groups.

The Knowledge Revolution

We live in a period of major structural change. The classic industrial revolution that started in the United Kingdom at the end of the eighteenth century spread gradually and unevenly to Europe and beyond. By the end of the twentieth century, a number of so-called follower countries had joined the ranks of industrial nations, and today industrial countries are found throughout the world. Some have narrowed, and even closed, the gap between rich and poor, with the East Asian countries being a good example. Average incomes have tended to increase across the world (except in Sub-Saharan Africa) in the past 20 years, although one-quarter of the world's population still lives in abject poverty.

In a predominantly industrial economy, the economic processes involved in catch-up are well understood. Levels of agricultural and manufacturing productivity must be raised by combining imported technology from advanced countries with relatively cheap labor, and by moving labor from low- to high-productivity sectors. In this traditional pattern of development, an educated (and healthy) labor force is a great advantage, but the emphasis is on basic literacy and numeracy skills, and the capacity to learn new tasks.

This pattern is still valid, but the late twentieth century saw the growth of a knowledge-centered, as opposed to a manufacturing-centered, economy. The "knowledge revolution" has seen exponential and continuing increases in knowledge in advanced countries since World War II. Many indicators confirm this, including the number of new patents, databases, and journals, as well as research and development expenditures. Nearly all industries have been affected, from biotechnology to financial services, with the nature of economic growth changing since "tinkerers" and craftsmen guided the early technology of the industrial revolution. Systematic knowledge has gradually replaced experience in furthering technology, with sophisticated and theoretical knowledge now the predominant path for technical progress. The world's Silicon Valleys are pushing the technological envelope; they are doing so by building on a thorough understanding of the underlying science.

Advances in information technology, meanwhile, have made this ever-increasing volume of knowledge more accessible, effective, and powerful. Networked computers and new forms of telecommunications spread information around the world with dazzling speed. The Internet, in particular, means that more knowledge than ever is in circulation. Those who have the skills to use it have access to an extraordinarily valuable (and sustainable) resource.

Participation in the knowledge economy requires a new set of human skills. People need to have higher qualifications and to be capable of greater intellectual independence. They must be flexible and be able to continue learning well beyond the traditional age for schooling. Without improved human capital, countries will inevitably fall behind and experience intellectual and economic marginalization and isolation. The result will be continuing, if not rising, poverty.

As *Knowledge for Development,* the 1998–99 *World Development Report,* puts it: "Knowledge is like light. Weightless and intangible, it can easily travel the world, enlightening the lives

Into the Heart of the Matter—The Travails of Higher Education in the Democratic Republic of the Congo (DRC)

Like most developing countries, the DRC faces powerful pressures to expand its higher education sector. After achieving independence from Belgium in 1960, what is now the third largest African country, with a current population of 47 million, had only two universities, both established in the mid-1950s. Their combined enrollment was around 2,000 students. Five years later, in 1965, enrollment in higher education—as a proportion of the number of people at the ages most relevant to higher education—had still barely moved above zero (as compared with the 4 percent average of both Asia and Latin America).

Both the government and private organizations have attempted to address the growing demand. The government established several pedagogical institutes designed to produce secondary school teachers. Continuing pressure for access to higher education has also led to the establishment of several private three-year institutes, as well as a few private universities offering, among them, degrees in medicine, the sciences, economics, international relations, law, politics, communications, humanities, and philosophy.

Despite these initiatives, demand continues to outstrip capacity. Acute shortages are evident in technology, the sciences, and medicine—fields in which training is particularly expensive to provide. The number of requests for enrollment in these fields is so high that during the academic year 1995–96, at the

Public University of Kinshasa, nearly 2,500 freshmen packed a single class in biomedical sciences. And students are right to seek to become physicians, given that the DRC has only one doctor for every 14,000 inhabitants. By 1995, the country continued to have an extremely low proportion of its population enrolled in higher education, compared to other developing countries. Moreover, most of the new schools replicate each other, and programs in medicine, technology, or specialized education remain rare.

The DRC, like many developing countries, faces the challenge of responding to increasing demand while attempting to provide a quality education. The current situation is extremely difficult. Most universities, public and private, lack the necessary funds to provide basic educational infrastructure—sufficiently spacious classrooms, laboratories, equipped teaching hospitals, libraries, computers, and Internet access. In general, students have no textbooks, and professors must dictate their notes or copy them onto a blackboard. The majority of schools have no library, no telephone, and not a single computer that students can use.

Schools in the DRC share a number of serious problems. The DRC as a whole lacks sufficient resources to provide adequate support to faculty. Many professors therefore choose either to teach at several universities to make ends meet, to move to corporations, or simply to relocate to a developed coun-

of people everywhere. Yet billions of people still live in the darkness of poverty—unnecessarily." In part, at least, people live in poverty because they cannot reach the switch to turn on the light, and that switch is called education. Higher education has never been as important to the future of the developing world as it is right now. It cannot guarantee rapid economic development—but sustained progress is impossible without it.

As the World Bank recognizes, the further developing countries fall behind, the more dif-

---

Box 1 continued

try for higher pay. Several factors help to foment corruption and undermine professors' willingness to evaluate students even-handedly, including low pay for faculty and salary payment delays lasting several months. The current evaluation system is highly subjective and leaves students at the mercy of professors who themselves often need to be evaluated.

Another critical issue is the shortage of faculty with graduate-level training. Most faculty are trained in overseas universities. The current scarcity of government resources and international scholarships for overseas universities makes it difficult to plan any significant training of future faculty to expand higher education. A plausible solution might begin with the establishment of a few graduate schools, in a variety of disciplines, through cooperation with international universities and foreign donors.

Another problem with higher education in the DRC is that it is rarely possible to study part-time. In the current official system, all students are registered for full-time attendance. Failing to pass any course automatically cancels all grades obtained that year, even for courses that a student has passed. This practice discourages working people from improving their skills and contributing to the nation's development. A rare exception is the American University of Kinshasa (Université Franco-Américaine de Kinshasa), a private university that since 1994 has pioneered a credit-based system that also allows students to program their courses around a work schedule.

Public universities in the DRC also need the restoration of managerial and financial autonomy (which they lost in 1972). Autonomy could promote quality education by stimulating competition, as was formerly the case between Université Lovanium, Université Officielle du Congo, and Université Libre de Kisangani. Government will still need to play an active role, overseeing the system and setting policies, standards, and regulations. In summary, the DRC is a textbook example of systemic problems that are fundamentally undermining the country's ability to capture the benefits of higher education.

Higher education involves more than teaching relevant skills to students. Theoretical and applied knowledge in a multitude of fields is created in universities, which also teach people how to access and use the world's knowledge. Developing countries need strong universities not only to carry out their own research, but also to select and absorb knowledge from all over the world. Undoubtedly other "green revolutions" will take place, and they are likely to be even more complicated and knowledge-intensive in their nature and application. Given the international setting of higher education—the worldwide community of scholars, study and training, and research reaching across borders—universities are ideally suited for the tasks of selection and absorption of knowledge.

ficulties they face. They are, it says, pursuing a moving target, as the high-income countries constantly push the knowledge frontier outward and pull away from the rest. At one time the rich countries might have viewed this future with indifference, confident that they were insulated from third-world misery. Today, with memories of the contagion that accompanied the first global financial crisis still fresh in people's minds, misery has become an infectious disease.

The new realities do not supersede the traditional goals of higher education, however. Indeed, there are many overlaps. Democracy, for instance, has spread at the same time as the knowledge revolution has gathered pace. It is founded both on well understood and widely practiced standards of civic virtue, and on the knowledge that allows widespread participation in the running of a society, values that can be examined and propagated in higher education institutions more effectively than they currently are.

Taken together, the new realities and traditional goals provide a powerful public-interest argument for developing higher education. The Task Force believes that the social returns to investment are substantial and exceed private returns by a wider margin than was previously believed.

Structure of the Report

Higher Education in Developing Countries: Peril and Promise is aimed at five key audiences:

- higher education policymakers, including education ministers, members of governing boards, and others, who need to understand the special needs and opportunities that higher education faces in the new century;

- the wider political community, especially ministers of the economy and ministers of industry, as well as business leaders whose support is vital to enabling higher education to reach its goals;

- higher education professionals, such as presidents, rectors, vice-chancellors, deans, and professors who are responsible for enacting reforms and creating institutions that provide a high-quality and efficient service;

- lenders and donors, who must decide how they can best support the enhancement of higher education in the developing countries; and

- the general public (including students), whose understanding and support are absolutely necessary, given the quantity of public and private resources consumed by higher education.

The report helps guide these audiences through both the older problems and new realities faced by higher education. It avoids treating in detail topics that have been fully and frequently examined by others, such as financing and the use of new technologies in education,[3] and concentrates instead on areas that have received little consideration, especially those that reflect new pressures on the system. Expansion, differentiation, and the knowledge revolution are discussed in

---

[3] On financing see, for example, D. Bruce Johnstone, "The Financing and Management of Higher Education: A Status Report on Worldwide Reforms," a paper supported by the World Bank in connection with the UNESCO World Conference on Higher Education, Paris, October 5-9, 1998; World Bank, *Higher Education: The Lessons of Experience,* 1994; and A. Ziderman and D. Albrecht, *Financing Universities in Developing Countries,* Washington, D.C./London: The Falmer Press, 1995. On technology see, for example, John S. Daniel, *Mega-Universities and Knowledge Media: Technology Strategies for Higher Education,* London: Kogan Page, 1996; and World Bank, *World Development Report 1998-99: Knowledge for Development,* New York: Oxford University Press, 1999.

detail, as are neglected topics of considerable current importance, such as the governance of higher education, the need to consider higher education as a system, and the public interest in higher education. We also include substantial discussions on improving science and technology research and instruction in institutions of higher education, and on the nature and importance of general education.

The report proceeds by reasoned argument, relying heavily on experience and belief. Some empirical support is provided from case studies and statistical analysis, although further data analysis would certainly be use-ful. Each chapter directs attention to a major issue in higher education, starting a dialogue from which we hope more specific policy recommendations will emerge. We have not attempted comprehensive studies of individual countries, or even of specific continents, but have instead addressed problems that affect many countries, cultures, histories, and traditions. We hope that each developing country, and each higher education institution, will find fresh insights in our work—and translate them into new ways of working in their own context.

Chapter 1

Longstanding Problems and New Realities

This chapter examines the current state of higher education in developing countries, and considers the new realities these countries face and how they are reshaping their response to ongoing challenges. In the past decades, developing countries have witnessed a rapid expansion of higher education, the simultaneous differentiation of higher education institutions into new forms, and the increasing importance of knowledge for social and economic development.[4] We focus on issues affecting most developing countries—exceptions exist, but should not affect the main thrust of our argument. In subsequent chapters, we explore the strategies and initiatives that are needed to meet these challenges.

The Current Situation

Higher education institutions clearly need well-designed academic programs and a clear mission. Most important to their success, however, are high-quality faculty, committed and well-prepared students, and sufficient resources. Despite notable exceptions, most higher education institutions in developing countries suffer severe deficiencies in each of these areas. As a result, few perform to a consistently high standard.

---

[4] We realize that the differentiation of higher education institutions is not a new phenomenon, as different types of colleges and universities have existed for centuries. What is new, however, is the strength of the forces driving differentiation, the pace at which it is occurring, and the variety of institutions being created.

Faculty Quality

A well-qualified and highly motivated faculty is critical to the quality of higher education institutions. Unfortunately, even at flagship universities in developing countries, many faculty members have little, if any, graduate-level training. This limits the level of knowledge imparted to students and restricts the students' ability to access existing knowledge and generate new ideas.

Teaching methods are often outmoded. Rote learning is common, with instructors doing little more in the classroom than copying their notes onto a blackboard. The students, who are frequently unable to afford a textbook, must then transcribe the notes into a notebook, and those students who regurgitate a credible portion of their notes from memory achieve exam success. These passive approaches to teaching have little value in a world where creativity and flexibility are at a premium. A more enlightened view of learning is urgently needed, emphasizing active intellectual engagement, participation, and discovery, rather than the passive absorption of facts.

Improving the quality of faculty is made more difficult by the ill-conceived incentive structures found in many developing countries. Faculty pay is generally very low in relation to that offered by alternative professional occupations. Pay increases are governed by bureaucratic personnel systems that reward long service rather than success in teaching or research. Market forces, which attempt to reward good performance, are seldom used to determine pay in the higher education sector.

While pay disparities make it difficult to attract talented individuals, recruitment procedures are often found to hinder intellectual growth. Some developing countries have been slow to develop traditions of academic freedom and independent scholarship. Bureaucracy and corruption are common, affecting the selection and treatment of both students and faculty (see Chapter 4). Favoritism and patronage contribute to academic inbreeding that denies universities the benefit of intellectual cross-fertilization. These problems arise most commonly in politicized academic settings, where power rather than merit weighs most heavily in the making of important decisions.

Politicization can also have a wider impact on the atmosphere of a system. While political activity on campuses throughout the world has helped address injustices and promote democracy, in many instances it has also inappropriately disrupted campus life. Research, teaching, and learning are extremely difficult when a few faculty members, students, and student groups take up positions as combative agents of rival political factions.

Higher education institutions rely on the commitment of their faculty. Their consistent presence and availability to students and colleagues have an enormous influence in creating an atmosphere that encourages learning. Yet few institutions in developing countries have strictures against moonlighting and excessive absenteeism. Many faculty work part-time at several institutions, devote little attention to research or to improving their teaching, and play little or no role in the life of the institutions employing them. Faculty members are often more interested in teaching another course—often at an unaccredited school—than in increasing their presence and commitment to the main institution with which they are affiliated. With wages so low, it is difficult to condemn such behavior.

Problems Faced by Students

In many institutions, students face difficult conditions for study. Severely overcrowded classes, inadequate library and laboratory facilities, distracting living conditions, and few, if any, student services are the norm. The financial strains currently faced by most universities are making conditions even worse.

Many students start their studies academically unprepared for higher education. Poor basic and secondary education, combined with a lack of selection in the academic system, lie at the root of this problem. Yet rarely does an institution respond by creating remedial programs for inadequately prepared students.

Cultural traditions and infrastructure limitations also frequently cause students to study subjects, such as humanities and the arts, that offer limited job opportunities and lead to "educated unemployment." At the same time, there is often unmet demand for qualified science graduates (see Chapter 5), while in many societies women study subjects that conform to their traditional roles, rather than courses that will maximize their opportunities in the labor market. Better information on the labor market is needed, combined with policies that promote economic growth and labor absorption. Also, many educated people come from wealthier backgrounds and are able to resist taking jobs in locations they consider to be undesirable. Promoting an entrepreneurial culture will encourage the creation of more productive jobs.

Students also face the widespread requirement to choose their area of specialization early in their course, in some cases ahead of matriculation. Once a choice is made, change is frequently difficult or even impossible. Such inflexibility closes off options, with students unable to sample courses in different academic areas. Early specialization can prevent costly indecisiveness, but systems that are unforgiving of early "mistakes" do not develop and unleash the true potential of many students.

Insufficient Resources and Autonomy

Many of the problems involving higher education are rooted in a lack of resources. For example, developing countries spend far less than developed countries on each student. But finding new funds is not easy. Although absolute spending is low, developing countries are already spending a higher proportion of their (smaller) incomes than the developed world on higher education, with public spending for education growing more quickly than income or total government spending. Higher education is clearly placing greater demands on public budgets,[5] with the private sector and international donors taking up only some of the slack. Redirecting money from primary or secondary education is rarely an option, with spending per student on higher education already considerably higher than is common at other levels of the education system.

Most public universities are highly dependent on central governments for their financial resources. Tuition fees are often negligible or nonexistent, and attempts to increase their level encounter major resistance. Even when tuition fees are collected, the funds often bypass the university and go directly into the coffers of ministries of finance or central revenue departments. Budgets must typically be approved by government officials, who may have little understanding of higher education in general, of the goals and capabilities of a particular university, or of the local context in which it operates.

In addition, capital and operating budgets are poorly coordinated. Often, major new facilities are built, but then are left with no funds for operation and maintenance. The developing world is littered with deteriorating buildings, inadequate libraries, computer laboratories that are rarely open, and scientific equipment that cannot be used for want of supplies and parts. It is often impossible to carry over unspent funds for use in later years, and difficult to win a budget that is higher than the previous year's actual expenditure. This creates a "use-it-or-lose-it environment," resulting in overspending and misspent resources.

Research universities face an array of especially serious problems. Their role derives from a unique capacity to combine the generation of new knowledge with the transmission of existing knowledge. Recent pressures to expand higher education, discussed at length below, have in many cases diverted such universities from pursuing research, and their financial situation is further diminishing their research capabilities. Public universities in Africa and Asia often devote up to 80 percent of their budgets to personnel and student maintenance costs, leaving few resources for infrastructure maintenance, libraries, equipment, or supplies—all key ingredients in maintaining a research establishment.

The disappearance of a research agenda from these universities has serious consequences. The inability to pursue research isolates the nation's elite scholars and scientists, leaving them unable to keep up with developments in their own fields. As research universities lose their ability to act as reference points for the rest of the education system, countries quickly find it harder to make key decisions about the international issues affecting them.

In addition to being severely underfunded, sometimes despite their best efforts, many higher education institutions in developing

---

5 A lack of data on education costs prevents inferences about whether these increased expenditures imply quality changes.

countries lack the authority to make key academic, financial, and personnel decisions. They can also be slow to devolve responsibility for decisionmaking to constituent departments. Poor governance, in other words, dilutes their ability to spend what money they have.

Expansion of Higher Education Systems

Problems of quality and lack of resources are compounded by the new realities faced by higher education, the first of which is *expansion*, as higher education institutions battle to cope with ever-increasing student numbers. Responding to this demand without further diluting quality is an especially daunting challenge.

Precursors

Over the past 50 years educational development has focused on expanding access to primary education. Starting from a low base, the results have been extraordinary. In 1965, less than half the adult population of developing countries was literate—less than one-third in Sub-Saharan Africa and South Asia. By 1995, however, 70 percent of adults living in developing countries were literate, with literacy levels above 50 percent even in Sub-Saharan Africa. Primary school enrollments have skyrocketed, with variations in performance between rich and poor countries shrinking rapidly (see Figure 2).

As increasing numbers of students complete primary school, demand for access to

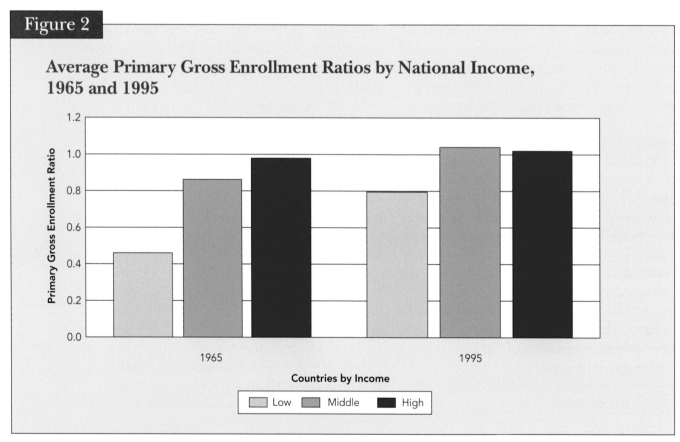

Figure 2

Average Primary Gross Enrollment Ratios by National Income, 1965 and 1995

Note: Countries are shown according to income groups as defined by the World Bank. The gross enrollment ratio can exceed 100 percent. See definition in Statistical Appendix. Source: Robert Barro and Jong-Wha Lee, *Data Set for a Panel of 138 Countries*, 1994; UNESCO, Division of Statistics, http://unescostat.unesco.org, March, April, and May, 1999; United Nations, *World Population Prospects 1950–2050*, electronic data set: *Demographic Indicators 1950–2050*, 1996.

secondary education rises. In recent decades, secondary enrollment ratios have increased significantly, and further expansion is almost certain. For example, between 1965 and 1995 the secondary gross enrollment ratio[6] increased from 16 to 47 percent in Brazil, from 5 to 32 percent in Nigeria, and from 12 to 30 percent in Pakistan. This has a double impact on higher education. More secondary students would mean more people entering higher education, even if the proportion progressing remained constant. However, the proportion who do want to graduate to higher education is increasing substantially, as globalization makes skilled workers more valuable and the international market for ideas, top faculty, and promising students continues to develop.

The substantial widening of access to primary and secondary education has combined with two other factors to impel the expansion of the higher education system: (i) a rapid increase in the number of people at the traditional ages for attending higher education institutions,[7] and (ii) a higher proportion of secondary school graduates progressing to higher education. Demographic change, income growth, urbanization, and the growing economic importance of knowledge and skills have combined to ensure that, in most developing countries, higher education is no longer a small cultural enterprise for the elite. Rather, it has become vital to nearly every nation's plans for development.

As a result, higher education is indisputably the new frontier of educational development in a growing number of countries (Figure 3). The number of adults in developing countries with at least some higher education increased by a factor of roughly 2.5 between 1975 and 1990. In 1995 more than 47 million students were enrolled in higher education in the developing world, up from nearly 28 million in 1980. For most developing countries, higher education enrollments are growing faster than their populations, a trend that will continue for at least another decade.

This continued expansion of higher education is clearly necessary to meet increased demand. However, it has brought with it some new problems. For example China, India, Indonesia, the Philippines, and Russia now have systems of higher education serving 2 million or more students. A further seven developing countries—Argentina, Brazil, Egypt, Iran, Mexico, Thailand, and Ukraine—enroll between 1 and 2 million students. To accommodate so many students, some institutions have had to stretch their organizational boundaries severely, giving birth to "mega-universities" such as the National University of Mexico and the University of Buenos Aires in Argentina, each of which has an enrollment of more than 200,000 students.

Expansion, both public and private, has been unbridled, unplanned, and often chaotic. The results—deterioration in average quality, continuing interregional, intercountry, and intracountry inequities, and increased for-profit provision of higher education—could all have serious consequences.

Imbalances

Although higher education enrollment rose sharply between 1980 and 1995 in both industrial and developing countries, the enrollment rate in industrial countries has remained roughly five to six times that of developing countries.

Within countries there are major imbalances between urban and rural areas, rich and poor households, men and women, and among ethnic groups. We know of no coun-

---

[6] See Statistical Appendix, Part II, Selected Definitions, for definition.

[7] There is nothing ephemeral about this trend. Demographic projections show that the number of 20- to 24-year-olds will continue to increase rapidly in many developing countries over the next decade.

Figure 3

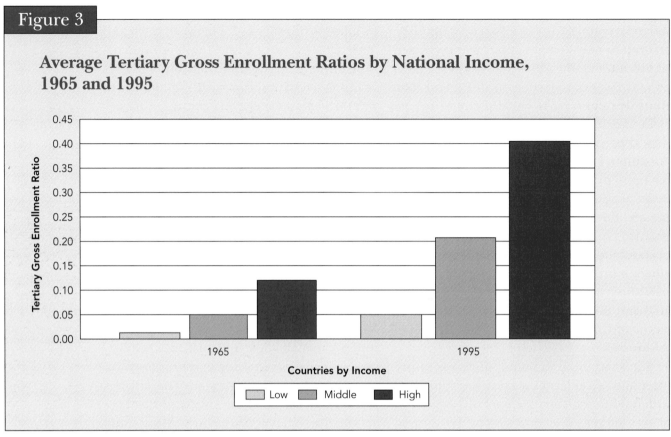

Average Tertiary Gross Enrollment Ratios by National Income, 1965 and 1995

Note: Countries are shown according to income groups as defined by the World Bank. The gross enrollment ratio can exceed 100 percent. See definition in Statistical Appendix. Source: Robert Barro and Jong-Wha Lee, *Data Set for a Panel of 138 Countries*, 1994; UNESCO, Division of Statistics, http://unescostat.unesco.org, March, April, and May, 1999; United Nations, *World Population Prospects 1950–2050*, electronic data set: *Demographic Indicators 1950–2050*, 1996.

try in which high-income groups are not heavily over-represented in tertiary enrollments. For example, in Latin America, even though the technical and professional strata account for no more than 15 percent of the general population, their children account for nearly half the total enrollment in higher education, and still more in some of the best public universities such as the University of São Paulo and the University of Campinas in Brazil, the Simón Bolivar University in Venezuela, and the National University of Bogotá in Colombia.

Between 1965 and 1995, the female share of enrollment in higher education in the developing world increased from 32 to 45 per-cent. Female enrollment is driving nearly half of the increased demand for higher education, and will presumably promote greater gender equality. But at present, outside the industrial countries only Latin America and the countries in transition have achieved overall gender balance.

Differentiation of Higher Education Institutions

Not only have higher education systems expanded worldwide, the nature of the institutions within these systems has also been shifting, through a process of differentiation.

Differentiation can occur vertically as the types of institutions proliferate, with the traditional research university being joined by polytechnics, professional schools, institutions that grant degrees but do not conduct research, and community colleges. Differentiation can also occur horizontally by the creation of new institutions operated by private providers, such as for-profit entities, philanthropic and other nonprofit organizations, and religious groups. The spread of distance-learning operations is an increasingly important example of differentiation and has both vertical and horizontal features.

Private education in developing countries has been growing since the 1960s. Not all of this growth has been in for-profit institutions: private philanthropic institutions have also been expanding. These are not-for-profit institutions that rely on a combination of gifts and fees. Philanthropic institutions have played a particularly significant role in providing high-quality education, although narrowly defined and strongly rooted objectives can limit the extent to which many of these institutions are able to advance the wider public interest. Philanthropic institutions generally fall somewhere between public and for-profit institutions, sharing some of the strengths, weaknesses, and objectives of each. In many contexts the distinction between for-profit and not-for-profit private institutions is of greater practical significance than the more traditional division between public and private institutions, since not-for-profit private institutions frequently resemble public institutions in terms of their mission and their structure.

Horizontal Differentiation

The growth of private higher education institutions, especially for-profit institutions, is the most striking manifestation of differentiation. Although the exact scale of private expansion is difficult to determine, the number of private institutions increased dramatically in many parts of Asia and Africa from the 1980s onwards—a process that started much earlier in Latin America, where institutions with religious affiliations are strong.

China now has more than 800 private higher education institutions, although the Ministry of Education officially recognizes only a handful of them. Nearly 60 percent of Brazil's tertiary-level students are currently enrolled in private institutions, which comprise nearly 80 percent of the country's higher education system. At independence in 1945 Indonesia had only 1,000 tertiary-level students. It now has 57 public universities and more than 1,200 private universities, with more than 60 percent of the student body enrolled in private institutions. In South Africa, roughly half of the country's students are enrolled in private institutions (see Figure 4).

This trend seems certain to continue. Deregulation in many countries is loosening the state's grip on the founding and operation of private institutions. Where demand has built up, growth is likely to be especially strong. A growing private sector does not necessarily lead to increased diversity, as new universities may simply imitate the curricular offerings of the public universities (as has tended to happen in Latin America). In general, though, new private institutions are likely to be somewhat innovative, if only because they do not have an institutional history to overcome. The ability to respond to the market and greater legal freedom may also be important. Private universities in South Asia, for example, have introduced innovations in the form of the semester system, standardized examinations, and credit systems.

The creation of new universities by religious organizations is a particularly important phenomenon. For example, the United Methodist Church established the African University in Zimbabwe, with department heads selected

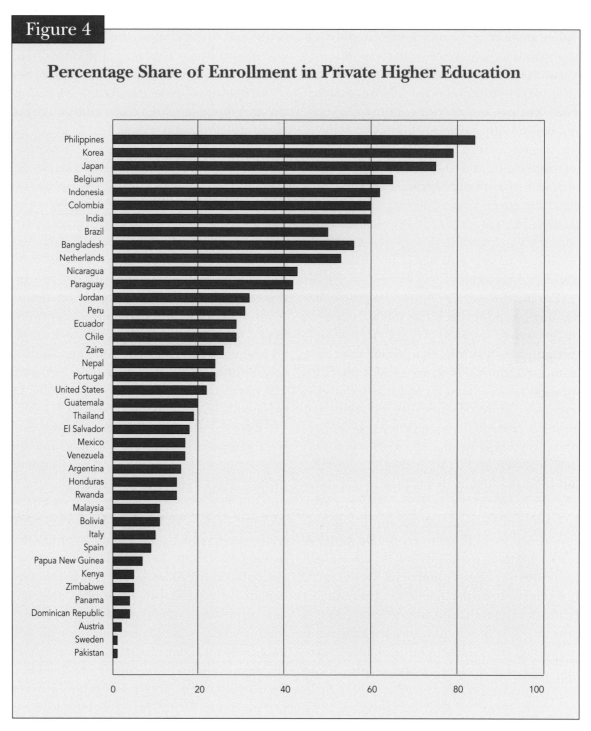

Figure 4

Percentage Share of Enrollment in Private Higher Education

Note: In Japan and the few Western European countries that have a high proportion of enrollments in private institutions (for example, Belgium and the Netherlands), higher education continues to be almost entirely financed by the state, which subsidizes both public and private higher education institutions. Source: World Bank, *Higher Education: The Lessons of Experience*, 1994.

from among nationals of different African countries. Well-established religious universities—Protestant, Catholic, and Muslim—operate in Kenya, Tanzania, and Uganda. A similar phenomenon involving Catholic universities occurs in Latin America.

Distance learning, in which students take classes primarily via radio, television, or the Internet, has expanded enormously during the past decade. (Both Nelson Mandela and Robert Mugabe earned their degrees in this way, at the world's oldest distance-learning university, the University of South Africa.) The five largest programs in the world are all based in developing countries, and all of these have been established since 1978 (see Table 1). They claimed an aggregate enrollment of roughly 2 million students in 1997, and account for about 10 percent of enrollment growth in developing countries during the past two decades. Educators have long been using radio and television to reach students in remote areas, but new satellite- and Internet-based technologies promise to extend distance-learning systems to a broader group of students, ranging from those in sparsely populated, remote areas to those living in dense urban agglomerations. In the United States, for example, the University of Phoenix is vigorously promoting its online courses, while in the United Kingdom, the publicly funded Open University has over 100 courses that use information technology links as a central part of the teaching—with 4,000 students per day connecting via the Internet.

Distance learning has great potential in the developing world, offering a powerful channel for bringing education to groups that have previously been excluded. In the future it is almost certain to take place increasingly across

Table 1   Ten Largest Distance-Learning Institutions

Institution	Founded	Students[a]	Budget (million US$)	Unit cost[b] (percent)
Anadolu University, Turkey	1982	578,000	30[c]	10
China TV University	1979	530,000	1[d]	40
Universitas Terbuka, Indonesia	1984	353,000	21	15
Indira Gandhi National Open University, India	1985	242,000	10	35
Sukhothai Thammathirat Open University, Thailand	1978	217,000	46	30
Korean National Open University	1982	211,000	79	5
National Centre for Distance Learning, France	1939	185,000	56	50
The Open University, Britain	1969	157,000	300	50
University of South Africa	1873	130,000	128	50
Payame Noor University, Iran	1987	117,000	13	25

[a] Figures are for 1994, 1995, or 1996.
[b] Cost per student as a percentage of average for other universities in that country.
[c] Open Education Faculty only.
[d] Central unit only.

Note: The figures in the accompanying table are the best available, but we recognize that many uncertainties arise in dealing with these and other cross-country comparisons. Source: John S. Daniel, *Mega-Universities and Knowledge Media: Technology Strategies for Higher Education*, London: Kogan Page, 1996, as cited by Dennis Normile, "Schools Ponder New Global Landscape," *Science*, 277, July 18, 1997.

borders. Already over 12 percent of the United Kingdom's Open University students are resident outside the country. It is also easy to conceive of high-quality developing country institutions offering educational programs and degrees in other parts of the developing world. While a desirable development, this would create a variety of problems relating to quality control and other forms of supervision.

Vertical Differentiation

While horizontal differentiation is driven by increased demand for higher education, vertical differentiation is a reaction to demand for a greater diversity of graduates. In general, economic development is associated with a more refined division of labor, and higher education institutions have an essential role to play in imparting necessary skills. The increasing importance of knowledge makes this range of skills in wider demand than ever. Today's developing economy needs not only civil servants, but also a whole host of other professionals such as industrial engineers, pharmacists, and computer scientists. Higher education institutions are adapting and new ones are emerging to provide training and credentials in new areas. As societies accept modern medicine, for example, they establish not only medical schools, but also schools of pharmacy.

The labor market also creates a demand for graduates who have undergone training of different types and intensities. Both public and private institutions have responded by creating academic programs that accommodate students with a wider range of capabilities. Some new programs allow students to earn lower-ranking degrees relatively quickly. In Bangladesh, some universities have two streams of undergraduate students: one that is admitted for a standard three-year bachelor's program, and another that is ad-

mitted to a less demanding two-year program. Both groups take the same classes, with less-advanced students having to complete fewer courses to graduate. As enrollments increase, new specialties can develop, attracting the critical mass of students and faculty that allow institutions to set up new departments, institutes, and programs.

Differentiation is spurred on by the relaxation of state regulations, but this poses serious quality problems. The argument that market forces will ensure suitable quality is simplistic. Private institutions often receive public subsidies through tax deductions on financial contributions or donations of physical facilities from public sources, or by accepting students whose tuition is financed by the government. To the extent that competition is driven by cost alone, it is likely to abet the provision of low-quality education. So-called garage universities sometimes disappear as quickly as they appeared, leaving students with severe difficulties in establishing the quality of their credentials.

Knowledge Acceleration

The expansion and differentiation of higher education is occurring at the same time as the pace of knowledge creation is dramatically accelerating. The categories into which new knowledge falls are becoming increasingly specialized, and a revolution has occurred in people's ability to access knowledge quickly and from increasingly distant locations. These changes are fundamentally altering what economies produce, as well as where and how they produce it. Organizations are changing, as are the skills needed to run them and the way they utilize human capital.

Industrial countries have been by far the greatest contributors to, and beneficiaries of, this knowledge revolution. To the extent that this trend continues, the income gap between industrial and developing countries will widen further. Higher education institutions, as the prime creators and conveyors of knowledge, must be at the forefront of efforts to narrow the development gap between industrial and developing counrtries.

Characteristics of the Revolution

The knowledge revolution can be described in a few key dimensions.

- Worldwide, the rate at which scientific papers are published has doubled in the past two decades. In economies where scientific capacity is expanding particularly rapidly, such as China, Hong Kong, Singapore, South Korea, and Taiwan, the publication rate has more than doubled in the past decade. The number of academic journals is now doubling roughly every five years, with new titles reflecting increasingly narrow specialties.

- In both industrial and developing countries, the number of patent applications has been increasing steadily. For example, in 1996 residents of Brazil, India, and the United States filed 42, 66, and 71 percent more patent applications, respectively, than in 1986.

- A country ranking of published scientific papers per capita during 1981–94 does not include a single developing country among the top 15. China and India make the list when assessed in terms of the absolute number of papers published, but this is due mainly to the sheer size of their populations.

- To a large extent the knowledge revolution has been driven by the use of personal computers and the Internet. However, as of 1996 industrial countries had about 20 times as many personal computers per capita as middle-income countries (224 versus 12 per 1,000 people) and more than 100 times as many Internet hosts (203 versus approximately 2 per 10,000 people).

The spectacular advances in recent decades in computerization, communications, and information technology have greatly enhanced the ability of researchers and entrepreneurs to create new knowledge, products, and services. Developments in electronics and computerization in the 1950s and 1960s laid the groundwork for incorporating microprocessors into a totally unanticipated array of devices, thereby transforming old machines into newly "smart" ones, while creating new machines at a breathtaking pace. New services have proliferated, transforming labor-intensive tasks such as managing payroll and travel reservation systems into technology-based activities. Factory production is increasingly based on robotics and sophisticated computer controls. Even automobile mechanics use computer-based analytical tools.

In recent years advances in communications and information technology have taken center stage. Fax machines have turned many isolated offices into active nerve centers, only to be superseded by electronic mail. Massive databases have consolidated huge quantities of information in one place, thereby allowing academics, entrepreneurs, and the general public to tap into them conveniently and rapidly. Most recently, the Internet has allowed people to access information about an unprecedented number of topics virtually instantly and, in most cases, cheaply. One of the factors underlying these changes is a dramatic reduction in the cost and ease of transmitting data. It will soon be possible to transmit 100 times as much data, for approximately one-hundredth the cost, as in 1983.

Beyond all these advances lie revolutions in other fields. New techniques in genetics and molecular biology have made possible new products, therapies, and cures, all of which promise to transform radically the quality of life. Chemists, physicists, and engineers have created new materials and processes, propelling plastics and ceramics into the heart of industrial operations and adopting fiber optics as the lifeblood of international communication. These changes are also creating formidable new geopolitical, ethical, legal, and human rights issues related to, for example, the development of new weapons, the possibilities inherent in cloning, and the threat to privacy posed by centralized databases and their phenomenal reach.

Implications for Developing Countries

The increasing importance of knowledge, in conjunction with the fact that most developing countries are falling further behind in their ability to create, absorb, and use it, has some major implications for developing countries.

- Countries that are only weakly connected to the rapidly emerging global knowledge system will find themselves increasingly at a disadvantage. The gap between industrial and developing countries in per capita incomes and standards of living will widen unless the corresponding gaps in knowledge and access to knowledge are successfully addressed.

Box 2

What If You Are Very Small?

The Maldives is a country of just 275,000 inhabitants scattered throughout the island atolls at the southernmost rim of India. With such a small population, the country faces a problem of how to administer higher education. Currently there are eight higher education institutions in the capital offering courses in health, education, technical education, hotel and catering, administration, law, and maritime training, in addition to a distance-learning center. They all fall under the umbrella of the Maldives College of Higher Education (MCHE) and each has branches in the atolls. Currently MCHE does not grant degrees, but over time it will evolve into a degree-granting institution. The problems faced by the Maldives are typical of small-island states, and include diseconomies of scale, mainly due to a scattered population; severe shortages of local, educated labor to staff post-secondary institutes; over-reliance on overseas education and training for all degree programs; and a lack of capacity to conduct applied research. These problems are serious and will take time to address.

However, international developments in distance learning and link programs offer true potential to bypass these critical capacity gaps. Access to international distance learning will be tried and closely linked to foreign university programs. For this to happen, accreditation standards and entrance qualifications of applicants have to rise and collaborative assistance needs to be worked out with associated institutions. On the whole, the Maldives is pinning its hopes on advanced telecommunications networks that will eventually make life-long learning inexpensive, even in remote islands.

In summary, the Maldives is experimenting with education that meets local needs. The issue is not whether the Maldives needs a traditional university, but rather how best to shape and deliver systems that provide high-quality, accredited courses to students across the country.

- Within countries, inequality will probably rise as some individuals and groups use their education (particularly higher education) to gain access to the knowledge system and then translate that access into higher incomes.

- Rectifying this situation is critical, but not easy. Although higher education is the traditional venue for gaining advanced knowledge, in many countries a large proportion of secondary school graduates are ill prepared to continue their studies and join the knowledge-centered world. Remedial programs at some higher education institutions may help rectify this problem, but strenuous efforts to improve primary and secondary education, including an emphasis on using technology to gain new knowledge, will also be necessary.

- Compared with investment in the production of goods, investment in the production of new knowledge yields potentially higher economic returns, but entails higher risks. For example, designing and marketing the best computer-operating system in the world is enormously lucrative; the second- and third-best systems are far less profitable. This would surely not apply in the case of steel mills, oil refineries, or food-processing plants. The winner-takes-all character of investment in knowledge demands a high level of existing knowledge and skills even to enter the fray. Few developing countries possess this knowledge. In this way, the knowledge gap will effectively preclude many upper-middle-income developing countries from participating in, and enjoying the benefits of, a growing and highly profitable set of economic activities. This issue is less relevant to low- and lower-middle-income countries, whose focus will be on developing the capacity to access and assimilate new knowledge.

Implications for Higher Education

Knowledge has become a springboard for economic growth and development, making the promotion of a culture that supports its creation and dissemination a vital task. Policymakers must keep a number of considerations in mind.

- Students must learn not only what is known now, but also how to keep their knowledge up to date. New technology-based tools for gathering knowledge must become central elements of their education, and curricula should be designed so that students learn how to learn.

- Specialization is increasingly important. Institutions of higher education will need to provide opportunities for in-depth study of particular fields, while also (as we argue in Chapter 6) offering programs of general education that can serve as a solid foundation for life-long learning and later specialization.

- Institutional differentiation is a logical response to the increased specialization and importance of knowledge. In many cases, both new and reformed institutions can best serve the public interest by focusing on a well-defined set of goals for a particular set of students.

- Knowledge is being produced throughout the world, and active engagement with scholars in other countries is crucial for developing and maintaining a lively intellectual community. Much new knowledge is an international public good, and its benefits will extend well beyond the borders of the country in which it is created. Countries that allow information to flow freely will benefit more.

- The advances in communication and information technology that made such significant contributions to the knowledge revolution mean that emphasis on these fields is likely to pay dividends in a wide variety of areas.

Conclusions

In most developing countries higher education exhibits severe deficiencies, with the expansion of the system an aggravating factor. Demand for increased access is likely to continue, with public and private sectors seeking to meet it with an array of new higher education institutions. Rapid and chaotic expansion is usually the result, with the public sector generally underfunded and the private (for-profit) sector having problems establishing quality programs that address anything other than short-term, market-driven needs. A lack of information about institutional quality makes it difficult for students to make choices about their education, making it hard to enlist consumer demand in the battle to raise standards. Developing countries are left with a formidable task—expanding their higher education system and improving quality, all within continuing budgetary constraints.

Chapter 2 Higher Education and the Public Interest

For centuries people have gained a substantial benefit from the higher education they have received—and wider society has benefited too. This public interest is central to the argument that collective action is needed to support, nurture, and strengthen higher education institutions. It also affects decisions on how much should be invested in higher education and from what sources that investment should come.

It is good to keep in mind that *international support* for higher education has passed through three overlapping phases in the past half-century:

- general support to strengthen existing universities;

- an accelerated effort to establish a new type of higher education institution, the "development university," focused on serving local development needs, especially in the areas of agriculture, health, and industrial development; and

- various attempts to establish centers of excellence, especially in the areas of science and technology, but only in a very select group of countries.

These phases have had an uneven impact on universities over the decades and have gradually altered the way universities serve the public interest. This chapter explores the precise nature of the public interest in higher education and discusses why its importance has tended to be underestimated. It also explores the impact of the new realities—especially expansion and differentiation—on the strength of the public interest.

The Public Interest

Higher education simultaneously improves individual lives and enriches wider society, indicating a substantial overlap between private and public interests in higher education. Higher education raises wages and productivity, which makes both individuals and countries richer. It allows people to enjoy an enhanced "life of the mind," offering wider society both cultural and political benefits. And it can encourage independence and initiative, both valuable commodities in the knowledge society.

The benefits of education, according to the Inter-American Development Bank's *Facing up to Inequality in Latin America* (1999), for example, are substantial. In Latin America as a whole, a worker with six years of education earns 50 percent more than someone who has not attended school. This gap increases to 120 percent for those with 12 years of education (i.e., completing secondary school), and exceeds 200 percent for those with 17 years of education (i.e., completing a university diploma). These benefits are "private," although there are also public benefits, as a better trained workforce contributes to rising tax streams, better healthcare, improved institutional capital, and so forth.

The macroeconomic impact of education is strong: just as individuals with better education tend to achieve greater success in the labor market, so economies with higher enrollment rates and years of schooling appear to be more dynamic, competitive in global markets, and successful in terms of higher income per capita. The point is dramatically illustrated by the experience of East Asia. From 1991 to 1995, East Asia experienced faster growth per year than did Latin America. Economists calculate that the higher education levels of the East Asian workforce account for a full half-point of that difference. It is thus in the interests of a much wider set of policymakers, as well as the business community, to become more actively involved in national debates about the reform and future of education systems.

This chapter does not attempt to provide an exhaustive catalogue of areas where there is a public return to investments in higher education, above and beyond the private return. The intention is to illustrate the public-interest perspective as it relates to economic and social development, concentrating on higher education's ability to:

- unlock potential at all levels of society, helping talented people to gain advanced training whatever their background;

- create a pool of highly trained individuals that attains a critical size and becomes a key national resource;

- address topics whose long-term value to society is thought to exceed their current value to students and employers (for example, the humanities); and

- provide a space for the free and open discussion of ideas and values.

Developing countries are currently under great pressure to meet increased demand for higher education, and many are finding it hard to keep up. They are becoming increasingly reliant on fee-based education and private, for-profit providers. In this environment, education becomes more narrowly focused on providing a skilled labor pool for the immediate needs of the economy. Market forces predominate and the public benefits of—and responsibilities for—higher education recede from view.

Certainly, competition within the higher education sector can lead to higher standards and to significant benefits for individual students. In many developing countries, however, markets do not function well and this leads to a serious misallocation of resources. Access, for example, is limited by income, excluding potentially able students and diluting the quality of the student body. Poor market information dilutes competition, allowing weak, exploitative institutions—some of them foreign—to survive and even prosper, and lessening the chances of dynamic new entrants.

Even when markets work well and students receive a quality service, private institutions may still fail to serve the public interest. For-profit institutions must operate as businesses, facing the market test and trying to maximize the return on their investment. It may not make good financial sense for them to invest in public-interest functions, and therefore they may underinvest in certain subjects and types of higher education, even if these are important to the well-being of society as a whole. The public sector thus retains a vital and, in our opinion, irreplaceable role in the higher education sector.

This role can take many forms. Governments can be direct providers of higher education, offer finance for its provision, or do both. They can develop legal and regulatory institutions to promote and shape the higher education system, and regulate individual institutions—even when these are privately chartered and funded.

But governments do not have an open-ended mandate in this area. Whatever their policies, they must be able to demonstrate that they are using resources in a way that offers society benefits that the private sector cannot supply. The public interest argument cannot be a cover for public sector waste, inefficiency, or lack of vision.

The Influence of Rate-of-Return Analysis

Although the concept of human capital dates to Adam Smith's *Inquiry into the Nature and Causes of the Wealth of Nations* (1776), it is only within the past 50 years that labor economists have seriously examined the returns to investment in education. By the mid-1970s techniques focused on the difference between average annual earnings among people with different levels of educational attainment (for example, secondary versus primary school graduates). They also analyzed differences between social and private rates of return, by comparing the amount of public subsidy received by education with the amount of extra tax society was able to levy on resultant higher earnings.

These techniques seemed to demonstrate that higher education offered lower private returns than primary education. They also showed that social returns were lower and, considering that higher education absorbs considerably higher investment, they demonstrated that the public interest in higher education was substantially lower than that in primary education. Taken together, these results provided a powerful justification—especially for international donors and lenders—for focusing public educational investment at the primary level. This justification was further reinforced by the obvious gains in social equity associated with such a strategy, as highlighted and endorsed by the Jomtien Declaration in

1990. The World Bank drew the conclusion that its lending strategy should emphasize primary education, relegating higher education to a relatively minor place on its development agenda. The World Bank's stance has been influential, and many other donors have also emphasized primary and, to some extent, secondary education as instruments for promoting economic and social development.

The Task Force fully supports the continuation of large investment in primary and secondary education, but believes that traditional economic arguments are based on a limited understanding of what higher education institutions contribute. Rate-of-return studies treat educated people as valuable only through their higher earnings and the greater tax revenues extracted by society. But educated people clearly have many other effects on society: educated people are well positioned to be economic and social entrepreneurs, having a far-reaching impact on the economic and social well-being of their communities. They are also vital to creating an environment in which economic development is possible. Good governance, strong institutions, and a developed infrastructure are all needed if business is to thrive—and none of these is possible without highly educated people. Finally, rate-of-return analysis entirely misses the impact of university-based research on the economy—a far-reaching social benefit that is at the heart of any argument for developing strong higher education systems.

Access to Higher Education

An important ingredient in the public interest in higher education is its role in creating a meritocratic society that is able to secure the best political leaders and civil servants, doctors and teachers, lawyers and engineers, and business and civic leaders. These people are often selected from the most educated, and

The Basics of Rate-of-Return Analysis

Estimating the "rate of return" on investments in different levels of education allows public policymakers to judge the effectiveness of education policies that target different levels of the education system. Labor economists have a long tradition of constructing such estimates. One conventional approach involves comparing the average earnings of individuals at various stages of educational achievement (for example, those who have completed primary education versus those who have not, or those who have completed higher education versus those whose formal education ended with the completion of secondary school). After adjusting for direct costs associated with the corresponding levels of educational achievement (for example, tuition and fees), and taking account of the fact that the value of a given sum of money will vary depending on the time at which it is spent or received, the (discounted net) earnings differentials can be expressed in classic "rates-of-return" terms.

Rates of return are considered private if they are based on differences in take-home pay and the costs of schooling that come out of the pockets of students and their families. Standard references on the calculation of rates of return abound, with the leading collection of actual estimates reported by George Psacharopoulos, 1994 ("Returns to Investment in Education: A Global Update," *World Development*, 22: 1325–43).

Once both private and social rates of return are calculated, it is easy to calculate the difference in these rates—i.e., how much society benefits above and beyond the private return. It is this difference that provides an economic justification for government action. If the social return exceeds the private return, this tells us that the unfettered operation of private markets (so-called "laissez-faire") will not produce as much education as is desirable from the point of view of society. (This is because private markets base their decisions on private returns, whereas society should base its decisions on social returns.) Also, if the social rate of return to primary school exceeds that for higher education, this in turn suggests that primary school is a better social investment than higher education.

Such analyses were undertaken, and concluded that the difference was greater in primary education than in higher education, and therefore that government action was more justified in the former than in the latter. But the standard rate-of-return analyses stopped there, consistently failing to reflect that the benefits of higher education extend well beyond the incremental earnings accruing to those individuals who receive it.

an economy is less likely to develop when they are chosen from the richest, rather than the most talented. The Task Force challenges the notion that public investment in higher education is socially inequitable. This notion rests on the argument that university graduates constitute the future elite of society, and already have the advantage of tending to come from the better-off families and are thus not deserving of public subsidy. This argument overlooks two self-corrective tendencies. An educated and skilled stratum is indispensable to the social and economic development of a modern society, giving benefits to the society as a whole and not merely to those being educated. In addition, higher education has acted as a powerful mechanism for upward mobility in many countries, allowing the talented to thrive irrespective of their social origins.

Broadening access to higher education is an ongoing process and work still needs to be done. This should include helping disadvantaged groups to overcome the endemic problems that exclude them from the system.

Equally important is a careful examination of ways to reform tuition and fee structures that exclude candidates from poorer backgrounds. And finally, measures are required to stamp out corruption in awarding places in universities.

Problems Facing Women and Disadvantaged Groups

Disadvantaged groups—whether they are racial, linguistic, or religious groups in specific societies, or women almost everywhere—find it difficult to compete for places in the higher education system. They have usually received inadequate primary and secondary schooling, making further progression in the education system much harder to achieve. In some situations, for example with South Africa's African and colored populations and India's scheduled castes, the discrimination has been more direct, including concerted action to prevent groups from reaching universities or securing faculty appointments.

Even if attitudes toward disadvantaged groups have changed, their members still face systemic discrimination. For many years, certain groups have been poorly represented in higher education. This means that the faculty is likely to be unrepresentative of disadvantaged groups, and there will be real or perceived problems of institutional discrimination. A lack of role models can lead to groups concluding that higher education is "not for them."

Higher education is also reliant on the rest of the education system, and those who have received little primary or secondary education are clearly far less likely to progress to higher education. A long-term solution therefore requires public investment at all levels of the education system, in order that larger numbers of well-prepared candidates from disadvantaged groups can compete for access to higher education.

Higher education systems need to find a way of reconciling the dual values of excel-lence and equity. In an ideal society, excellence is best promoted by policies that select a society's most creative and motivated members for advanced education. But selection based on prior achievement will only reinforce a history of discrimination and underachievement. Equally, programs to increase equity will prove unsustainable if they are seen to undermine the standards of excellence on which higher education is based. Merit criteria cannot be relaxed. Awarding degrees or certificates to people who do not deserve them cannot be in the public interest.

The answer seems to be to combine tolerance at points of entrance with rigor at the point of exit. Proactive efforts to attract promising members of disadvantaged groups must be coupled with well-designed, consistently delivered remedial support. With sufficient funding from public or philanthropic funds, this will clearly contribute to equity, but it has the potential to contribute to excellence as well—with institutions drawing their intake from an ever-widening pool.

Tuition and Fee Structures

Well-prepared and talented students face difficulties in gaining access to higher education when the costs of education exceed their means. These costs include tuition fees, room and board, books and materials, and access to technology, as well as income that is foregone while attending school. This problem, which is of course particularly limiting at low income levels, is aggravated by the poor functioning of financial markets in many developing countries. This means that students cannot secure loans at reasonable rates to finance their schooling. Using public funds for scholarships, fellowships, or loan schemes, thereby lowering cost barriers for talented students who would otherwise be excluded, is economically sound and a time-honored function of public funds. In countries that have diversified systems of higher education, it is in the public interest to reduce cost barriers to private as well as to public institutions.

Corruption

With higher education offering such clear private benefits—both economic and social—corruption in the awarding of university places within some systems is unsurprising. Every higher education place awarded through corruption gives rise to the possibility that a less deserving candidate has been substituted for a more deserving candidate. If the problem is endemic, an educated class that fails to reflect the true distribution of aptitude and talent in the society will develop. Even minor instances of corruption are corrosive, increasing the possibility of disharmony within an institution and compromising its reputation.

Research and the Public Interest

One of the most powerful arguments for a public interest in higher education is the value to a country of a well-developed system for research and generation of knowledge. This is of increasing importance within the emerging knowledge economy, allowing a country not only to generate new knowledge, but also to engage in scholarly and scientific commerce with other nations.

Privately produced and held knowledge, whether based on military secrecy or commercial investment, has a role to play in society. However, basic research and fundamental knowledge generation thrive where new findings are widely shared and are available for testing and refinement within an open forum. Public support of knowledge generation is essential in developing countries.

Basic, nonproprietary research can be located in any number of institutions (national laboratories, government agencies, and private sector research institutes), but is especially well suited to universities and other higher education bodies. Research universities—most commonly public institutions—at least in principle integrate a number of practices that are highly conducive to knowledge generation. These include ideological neutrality in the selection of research topics, peer review and scholarly publication, close links between research and teaching, and the synergies that result from collecting the full range of disciplines in one institution (or integrated system of institutions).

A strong research system at the national level opens up the possibility that substantial additional public benefits can be realized through international links. Not all knowledge can or should be internally produced, when a worldwide system of basic knowledge production offers the classic economic benefits associated with specialization and exchange. International involvement helps countries guard against parochialism and remain open to broader economic, intellectual, technical, and social possibilities. Institutions of higher education, especially research universities, are particularly well equipped to facilitate the flow of new knowledge and to disseminate it internally once it is imported. Exchanges of both faculty and advanced students need to be facilitated, along with participation in international conferences and research projects. Nations must also act to remove legal restrictions on the flow of scholars and ideas, and ensure that there is adequate funding for this important work.

Publicly funded knowledge exchange also offers an international public good. Profit-based research is designed to capture and commercialize the benefits it generates, not to make them universally and freely available. In large measure, academic research stands outside these commercial transactions. Internationally, higher education is an intellectual commons represented by the invisible college of independent scholarship, knowledge production, and scholarly training. This intellectual commons allows the world to tackle a number of widely recognized international challenges: emergent diseases that move easily across national borders; invasive species that damage sites far removed from their point of origin; and climate fluctuations that disturb traditional growing seasons in widely scattered parts of the globe. In addition to these problems that migrate internationally, issues such as technology application or biodiversity protection emerge in a variety of settings and benefit from comparative examination.

It is difficult for any single nation to justify investing heavily in research focused on transnational problems, when other nations can benefit without having contributed. Creating this knowledge is in the public interest of all nations, but it needs supranational public investment if it is to be provided. A network of research universities and institutes is a natural mechanism for advancing the required research agenda. Public health and medical schools can collaborate on designing and managing a global surveillance system on emergent diseases, for example, while agricultural faculties and research institutes can do similar work on invasive species.

International knowledge exchange relies on each nation meeting international standards of higher education, both formal and informal. For example, a number of professions, including engineering, medicine, accounting, international law, and epidemiology, have developed performance standards that are generally recognized worldwide. Ensuring that the graduates of each nation's higher education system meet those standards allows those graduates to compete in international markets. It also allows nations to work on a level playing field with international agencies and multinational businesses. For example, negotiating the terms of structural adjustment policies necessitates a competence

in economics that matches that of the international donor community. Similarly, ensuring the effective operation of tradeable permit systems to mitigate global warming requires scientific competence within all the nations engaged in the trade regime. Attracting direct foreign investment relies on the ability to negotiate successfully with international business, which is likely to be attracted by a high-quality, professional workforce. It is the educated people of a nation, even of a poor nation, who will assert their nation's interest in the increasingly complex web of global economic, cultural, and political interactions. Without better higher education, it is hard to imagine how many poor countries will cope.

Improving higher education is therefore in every country's interest, and has legitimate claims on public funds. We also underscore the responsibility of international donors to redress current imbalances in research capacity across regions, so that every region can participate in international efforts to address key global challenges. Libraries are a crucial resource in this effort. Their improvement deserves urgent consideration, an initiative that could be greatly facilitated by advances in information technology.

The globalization of higher education can have damaging as well as beneficial consequences. It can lead to unregulated and poor-quality higher education, with the worldwide marketing of fraudulent degrees or other so-called higher education credentials a clear example. Franchise universities have also been problematic, where the parent university meets quality standards set in the home country but offers a substandard education through its franchised programs in other countries. The sponsoring institution, mainly in the United States or Europe, often has a "prestige name" and is motivated by pecuniary gain, not by spreading academic excellence to developing countries.

Higher Education and Democratic Values

Higher education has the additional role of reflecting and promoting an open and meritocratic civil society. Civil society is neither state nor market, but is a realm that links public and private purposes. Within this realm, higher education promotes values that are more inclusive or more "public" than other civic venues, such as religious communities, households and families, or ethnic and linguistic groups. Higher education is expected to embody norms of social interaction such as open debate and argumentative reason; to emphasize the autonomy and self-reliance of its individual members; and to reject discrimination based on gender, ethnicity, religious belief, or social class. The best higher education institution is a model and an impetus for creating a modern civil society. This is an ideal that is not often realized, but is nevertheless a standard against which to measure national systems.

More generally, a society that wishes to build or maintain a pluralistic, accountable democracy will benefit from a strong higher education sector in two respects: the first is the task of research and interpretation. A society's understanding of what form of political democracy will best suit it can be advanced on the basis of debates and research that start in universities and colleges. This is primarily the responsibility of the social sciences, but the humanities also have a key role to play. Higher education in the humanities is home to the most careful reasoning about the ethical and moral values important to that society. It joins the other disciplines in its respect for objectivity and for testing ideas against observation—with the experience of all societies, across history, upon which to draw.

Second, higher education helps to promote the enlightened citizens who are necessary for a democracy. It achieves this by instilling the norms and attitudes crucial to democracy in its own students, who then become the teachers, lawyers, journalists, politicians, and business leaders whose practices should promote enlightened citizenship across society. Higher education also contributes insofar as it demonstrates pluralism, tolerance, merit, reasoned argument, and other values that are as critical to democracy as they are to the educational process.

The deeper values promoted through higher education extend beyond those necessary for the design and preservation of democracy. Along with other cultural institutions, universities and colleges ensure that a society has a shared memory. This is important even if the memory is painful, as it is for societies trying to escape a racially or ethnically intolerant past, or a totalitarian and fearful history. Painful national memories, as much as celebratory and uplifting memories, constitute part of the culture from which the future is built. Higher education is a natural home for the study and teaching of history. It provides the research that in turn leads to a history and civics curriculum in primary and secondary school.

In pointing out these ambitious public responsibilities, the Task Force is not so naive as to presume that they are practiced always or everywhere. Higher education institutions have been home to moral cowardice as well as to moral courage. A critical social science was sustained in despotic Latin American countries only when its intellectual leaders fled universities and established independent research centers. Universities in South Africa collaborated with apartheid, and universities in Nazi Germany with anti-Semitism. Such instances of moral failure recur across time and place—not often, but often enough to remind us that universities have to earn the right of moral leadership.

Failures notwithstanding, societies have historically looked to higher education as a venue for reasoned discourse rather than partisanship, for tolerance rather than discrimination, for a free and open search for truth rather than secrecy or deception. For these reasons, universities are frequently the first targets of dictators.

To the extent that a higher education system meets these public expectations, it contributes to a set of values necessary for democratic practices to flourish. While it is, however, very difficult for universities and colleges to disconnect themselves from the politics and culture of their country, at best they aspire to reflect where their societies want to be, rather than where they are.

Conclusions

All types of higher education institutions—including those run for philanthropic and profit motives—can serve the public interest. The system as a whole needs to benefit from the vigor and interest of the market and the state. At the same time, it must not be dominated by either. Too close a reliance on mar-

ket forces reduces public benefits, a danger that may be magnified by the globalization of investment opportunities, thereby introducing priorities at odds with long-term national needs. However, the private benefits, both to individuals and in the aggregate, are a powerful and legitimate justification for higher education. No system of higher education should forego the advantages of the compelling logic of private investment for private benefit.

Equally, higher education must avoid being captured by the short-term partisan interests of the government in power, or being stymied by bureaucracy. This is not to dispute that the state has a legitimate interest in the quality and scope of higher education. This chapter emphasizes the need for state policies to protect and promote the public interest in higher education. But a critical principle of those state policies is sufficient autonomy for higher education. Subordination to government pressures or short-term political considerations will not create a system of higher education that serves the long-term interest of the public.

Chapter 3 Systems of Higher Education

The preceding chapters have made two central points. First, societies have a profound and long-term interest in their higher education institutions that extends beyond the pecuniary and short-term interests of current students, faculty, and administrators. Second, the current state of higher education in developing countries is generally quite weak. While globalization, technological and demographic changes, and the growing economic importance of knowledge are making higher education reform more urgent and challenging than in the past, some of these same factors are also making such reform potentially more attainable.

This chapter explores the web of public and private education institutions, governing bodies, and individuals that form a higher education system. It also examines the formal and informal rules that hold the web together, looking for the structure underlying what can appear to be a chaotic set of activities and entities. The Task Force believes that higher education needs to be developed in a coordinated way, guided by a clear strategic vision. We therefore go on to suggest guidelines for reforming higher education institutions so that they may be integrated more effectively as part of a system that efficiently meets national goals.

In the past, few academics or policymakers adopted a systems perspective when discussing higher education, which is why we devote a whole chapter to this topic. Analysts have tended to focus on individual institutions or on education systems as a whole. Although this is a sound approach in many circumstances, the nature of higher education differs fundamentally from primary and secondary education, and confers different benefits upon society. An examination of higher education systems in their own right can help to provide much needed guidelines for institutions regarding their roles and aspirations, to highlight society's interest in higher education, and to suggest specific policy mechanisms to advance that interest.

Outline of a Higher Education System

A higher education system consists of three basic elements:

- the individual higher education institutions (public and private, whether profit or non-profit; academic and vocational; undergraduate and graduate; onsite and distance-based, etc.), including their faculties, students, physical resources, missions, and strategic plans;

- the organizations that are directly involved in financing, managing, or operating higher education institutions, comprising a range of both public and private bodies; and

- the formal and informal rules that guide institutional and individual behavior and interactions among the various actors.

The system is not sealed from the outside world: it is at least loosely bound to the overall education system, for example, to secondary schools that provide most of its new students. It is connected to the labor market and the business community, and to various government departments that set the policy environment in which it operates. It also has international links, to regional and global higher education communities, as well as to bilateral and multilateral donors, foundations, and nongovernmental organizations. (Figure 5 graphically depicts a differentiated higher education system and its place in society.)

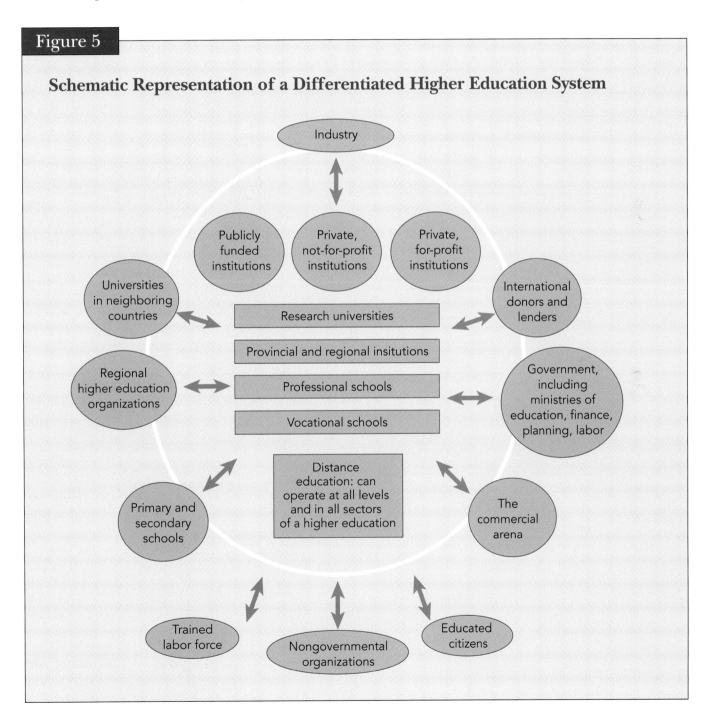

Figure 5

Schematic Representation of a Differentiated Higher Education System

Higher Education Institutions

As we have discussed, higher education across the world is undergoing a process of differentiation. This is happening horizontally as new providers enter the system, and vertically as institutional types proliferate. A diverse system, with a variety of institutions pursuing different goals and student audiences, is best able to serve individual and national goals. Recognizing the nature and legitimacy of this diversity helps ensure that there are fewer gaps in what the system can provide, while preventing duplication of effort. It is also helpful for halting institutional drift, where an institution loses focus on its "core business," failing to recognize that it is already serving a particular group of students well. In the case of mid-level institutions, if their crucial role is not understood they may try to gain prestige by moving up the educational hierarchy. This is unhelpful if it leaves a group of students poorly served and if the institutions are unable to function properly as they move upstream.

It is therefore useful to characterize the main types of institution that are typical within a higher education system. From the outset, we distinguish between public, private not-for-profit, and private for-profit institutions. To some extent, the objectives of these institutions—teaching, research, and service—overlap; so, too, does the autonomy they have to pursue those objectives. However, there are also fundamental differences. Notions of the public interest count more heavily in defining the mission of public institutions than of private ones. Public institutions also tend to be subject to greater bureaucratic control, which limits their autonomy. On the other hand, they are more buffered from market forces, giving them a greater measure of stability. State regulations do affect private institutions, but generally leave them with greater autonomy than public institutions experience in academic, financial, and personnel matters. All private institutions must cover their costs, but private, for-profit institutions also have the generation of a surplus as a core goal. These financial requirements impose considerable limits on their activities.

Research Universities

Research universities, which stand at the apex of the educational pyramid, tend to be public and certainly not for profit. Their overriding goals are achieving research excellence across many fields and providing high-quality education. They pursue these goals by having relatively light faculty teaching loads, emphasizing research accomplishments in recruitment and promotion decisions, adopting international standards for awarding degrees, and being highly selective in the students they admit. They are most closely connected to advances in knowledge, monitoring breakthroughs in many fields and investigating ways to exploit important results for social and private gain. Their instruction—generally for both first and post-graduate degrees—should be aimed at the country's most hard-working and best-prepared students. Research universities also have the capacity to offer the most complete programs of general education (see Chapter 6).

Provincial or Regional Universities

Institutions that focus predominantly on producing large numbers of graduates are another key component of a higher education system. They emphasize teaching and the training of "job-ready" graduates, especially those who can meet local skills requirements in areas such as manufacturing, business, agriculture, forestry, fisheries, and mining. They are commonly found in both the public and private sectors and tend to be geographically dispersed so that collectively they can cater to the many students who do not leave home to attend school. Provincial or regional universities often produce the majority of a country's graduates and tend to lie at the heart of the system's expansion. Some institutions offer two-year tertiary-level degrees, much like community colleges in many developed countries, offering another potential channel for providing mass higher education.

Professional Schools

Freestanding professional schools—and professional faculties in universities—provide training in fields such as law, medicine, business, and teaching, as well as other areas outside the jurisdiction of traditional arts and sciences faculties. These schools typically enroll students directly from high school and offer study programs that focus almost exclusively on technical training in the relevant area. Most developing countries have an urgent need for individuals with specialized professional skills, so professional schools play a critical role in national development, and often occupy a central place within developing country higher education systems. For-profit private institutions, in particular, can be directed into this area by market forces, concentrating on preparing students for careers with high private returns. Professional schools commonly pay little attention to providing a general education that would serve many students (and society) well.

Vocational Schools

Vocational schools operate in much the same way as professional schools, but at a different level. They endeavor to impart the practical skills needed for specific jobs in areas such as nursing, auto mechanics, bookkeeping, computers, electronics, and machining. They may be parallel to (or part of) the secondary education system, or part of the post-secondary

system, but they are not often considered a component of the higher education system per se. These schools, many of which are private and for-profit, play an important role in satisfying real labor-market demands.

Virtual Universities and Distance Learning

Distance learning is an increasingly important part of the higher education system, with its ability to reach students in remote areas and address the higher education needs of adults. It is not in itself a new idea—the University of South Africa, for example, has offered academic degrees through distance study for decades—but is growing at an astonishing rate (see Chapter 1 for data on the largest distance-learning institutions).

Distance learning can be offered by traditional educational institutions or by new institutions that specialize in this mode of study. While recent developments in communication technology and computers have vastly increased the technical viability of distance education, economic viability is still an issue in many countries because of costly and extensive infrastructure requirements. In many parts of Africa, for example, the telephone is still a luxury and long-distance calls are extremely expensive. Efficient distance learning will require affordable telephone and Internet access for this part of the world.

In the past, distance learning has been seen mainly as a cost-effective means of meeting demand, with policymakers paying inadequate attention to ensuring that it provides comparable quality to traditional modes of delivery. The Task Force believes that distance education offers many exciting possibilities. Innovative curricula can be combined with interactive, Internet-based technology, traditional educational media such as television and print, written materials, and direct contact with tutors. It needs, however, to be thoroughly integrated into the wider higher education system, subjected to appropriate accreditation and quality standards, and linked to the outside world. Research into how this can be achieved—and how distance learning can fulfil its potential—needs much greater attention.

Desirable Features of a Higher Education System

Effective systems of higher education tend to have a common set of characteristics. We suspect that many of these are prerequisites of any system that is functioning well, and find it difficult to identify any developing countries whose higher education systems would not benefit from an infusion of at least some of the characteristics (and related specific suggestions) discussed below.

Stratified Structure

Higher education systems are under great pressure to improve the quality of the education they offer—but also to educate increasing numbers of students. A stratified system is a hybrid that marries the goals of excellence and mass education, allowing each to be achieved within one system and using limited resources. A stratified system comprises one tier that is oriented toward research and selectivity and another that imparts knowledge to large numbers of students. It cements the distinction discussed above between research and provincial universities, allowing each to pursue clear objectives and avoid the duplication of effort. Stratified systems cater well to the varied nature of students' abilities and interests, and also allow for faculty with different skills to be best used. They are economical in terms of satisfying social needs, producing graduates who are able to fulfil a variety of roles and a generally educated citizenry. Finally, as specialized knowledge becomes in-

creasingly important to economic performance, they enable a higher education system to produce a mix of specialized and broadly trained graduates.

Policymakers need to be more explicit about expecting different contributions from different segments of a stratified system. Expressing a clear vision of the goals and structure of a higher education system is fundamental to setting an agenda for reform, while ensuring that this vision is widely shared is vital to achieving practical results.

Adequate and Stable Long-Term Funding

Higher education institutions can thrive only if their funding levels are adequate, stable and—subject to good performance—secure in the long term. Institutions must plan far ahead if they are to provide consistent instruction and a secure and productive work environment for their faculty. In many areas, insecure funding stifles the ability and the incentive to carry out research.

Governments have a crucial role to play in providing stability. They must finance public institutions on a long-term basis, not as if they were part of a nonessential government sector with the attendant vulnerability to the vagaries of fluctuations in public spending. They must also help create an environment conducive to the sustainable financing of private institutions and help the whole higher education system look to the future, ensuring that tomorrow's operating budgets will be sufficient to maintain and run the new infrastructure higher education will need.

Competition

Traditionally there has been little competition within higher education systems, and the Task Force believes that more intense competition between similar institutions for faculty, students, and resources will help improve standards by rewarding merit and performance. Competition also generally promotes beneficial innovations and overall quality improvements. Competition is exceedingly difficult to achieve through central decree, but requires a high degree of autonomy for academic institutions, allowing them to exploit their strengths and overcome weaknesses. Adequate market information is also essential: without it, institutions will continue to thrive even when they are weak.

One common indicator of competition is faculty mobility between institutions, which tends to promote a healthy academic environment through intellectual cross-fertilization. Too much competition is also possible, resulting in excessive faculty mobility and a lack of loyalty to institutions. However, most developing countries are a long way from experiencing this problem.

Flexibility

Higher education systems need to be flexible if they are to be most effective. They need to be able to adapt quickly to changing enrollment levels, to the rise and fall of different fields of study, and to changes in the mix of skills demanded in the labor market. Open systems are more likely to keep pace with significant external changes. Scholarly interaction within and between countries, frequent curriculum review, and strong connections to the world stock of knowledge (through substantial investments in Internet access, for example) are all important. Research is also useful. Basic demographic data can help forward planning, enabling institutions to prepare for changes in cohort size, secondary school enrollment, and graduation rates.

Well-Defined Standards

Effective higher education institutions articulate clear standards and set for themselves challenging goals that are consistent with the needs of their societies and labor forces. International standards are especially relevant in a globalized economy. Some standards are needed for degree requirements when it comes to student performance, faculty qualifications, and achievement. Mediocre institutions are not transformed into great institutions merely by announcing world-class standards: a realistic approach that concentrates on promoting achievable improvements is needed. A culture of accountability is also essential, allowing improvement (or deterioration) to be continually monitored and rewarded.

Immunity from Political Manipulation

Higher education systems are effective only when insulated from the undue influence of political parties, governments, or short-term political developments in educational affairs. Success in research and education requires consistency, with academic decisions—concerning institutional leadership, curriculum, or the funding of research projects—made for academic reasons. Excluding partisan political interests from the operation of a higher education system helps to safeguard meritocratic decisionmaking, one hallmark of an effective higher education system.

Well-Defined Links to Other Sectors

A higher education system does not operate in isolation. An effective system must pay attention to a country's secondary education system in order to take account of student preparation. It will also benefit primary and secondary education through training qualified teachers and demonstrating potential educational innovations. A quality system of higher education will also increase students' aspirations at the primary and secondary levels, leading to higher standards as students compete for tertiary education places.

Strong links between a country's higher education system and other systems both in the immediate region and beyond will have many beneficial effects, including significantly augmenting the resources available to an individual system, helping to overcome intellectual isolation, and allowing the achievement of "critical mass" in a larger number of specialized fields. In addition, a higher education system benefits from close coordination with other domestic public and private entities. For example, advocates for higher education and industry can work together to ensure that graduates have the skills that industry needs. Finally, advocates for higher education need to work comfortably with government agencies responsible for policy setting and finance.

Supportive Legal and Regulatory Structure

Higher education institutions flourish in a legal and regulatory environment that encourages innovation and achievement, while discouraging corruption, duplication of effort, and exploitation of poorly informed consumers. In many systems, initiative is stifled by counterproductive legal constraints and centralized decisionmaking. Higher education is focused on people—regulation needs to foster, not hamper, human potential.

System-Wide Resources

Many tools for improving higher education work best when developed centrally and shared widely. Such tools include management information systems, standardized tests, curriculum, and "knowledge banks" (repositories of information accessible through electronic means). They effectively and efficiently spread the financial and technical burdens of higher education development, allowing multiple institutions to work together.

The government, perhaps aided by inter-national donors, might also develop "learning commons"—a combination of computing centers, scientific laboratories, and libraries—accessible to students from all institutions of higher education, public and private. A learning commons would permit more effective use of outside higher education resources and permit some institutions to teach scientific subjects that they would not otherwise be able to offer. These commons would need to be located in strategic places throughout the country and be adequately maintained and staffed. They could also serve as focal points for public information, and contribute in this way to strengthening civil society.

Technology is an especially important system-wide resource. The past few decades have seen an explosion of technological capacity in both the industrial and developing worlds. No system of higher education can hope to serve its students, or the national interest, without developing a robust technological capacity. Higher education systems need to encourage all constituent institutions, both public and private, to incorporate advances in computing and communications technology into their administrative structures, their teaching, and their research. Integrating computers into learning is a key task if graduates are to be prepared for the jobs of the future. Students can also benefit tremendously from CD-ROM-based and Web-based curricula, which have the potential to bring high-quality educational materials to all parts of the developing world. Moreover, using the Internet as a means for gathering knowledge connects students and researchers to the worldwide community of scholars, an invaluable step in overcoming intellectual isolation.

The Task Force recognizes that acquiring access to such technology can be prohibitively expensive. International donors therefore have a particularly important role to play in this area. It is also important to ensure that importing technology does not create excessive reliance on education designed abroad. This issue raises serious concerns about cultural incompatibility and undue external influence. Developing countries need to maintain the unique character of their higher education systems, strengthening their intellectual self-reliance and making an important contribution to the diversity of the global community.

Role of the State

An effective system of higher education relies on the active oversight of the state. The government must ensure that the system serves the public interest, provides at least those elements of higher education that would not be supplied if left to the market, promotes equity, and supports those areas of basic research relevant to the country's needs. The state must also ensure that higher education institutions, and the system as a whole, operate on the basis of financial transparency and fairness. However, the government must also be economical in its interventions. It should only act when it has a clear diagnosis of the problem, is able to suggest a solution, and has the ability to apply this solution efficiently. Poorly-thought-through government action is likely to weaken already inadequate higher education systems.

The exact role of government in higher education has been subject to extensive debate, and can range from extreme state control to total laissez-faire. Under systems of state control, governments own, finance, and operate higher education institutions. Politicians frequently appoint vice-chancellors, and ministries dictate degree requirements and curricula. Many developing countries have gravitated toward this model in the postcolonial period, based on the rationale that governments are entitled to control systems that they fund. But state control of higher education has tended to undermine many major prin-

ciples of good governance. The direct involvement of politicians has generally politicized higher education, widening the possibilities for corruption, nepotism, and political opportunism.

Growing awareness of the disadvantages of state control has led many countries to adopt alternative models. State supervision aims at balancing the state's responsibility to protect and promote the public's interest with an individual institution's need for academic freedom and autonomy. So-called buffer mechanisms are important to achieving this balance. Buffer mechanisms generally consist of statutory bodies that include representatives of the government, institutions of higher education, the private sector, and other important stakeholders such as student organizations. Examples of buffer mechanisms would be:

- councils of higher education that advise the government on the size, shape, and funding of higher education; often they are also responsible for quality assurance, promotion mechanisms, and accreditation;

- research councils or agencies that fund and promote research;

- professional councils that focus on specific areas of higher education; and

- governing councils (or boards of trustees).

To be effective, these bodies require clear mandates, well-established operating procedures, and full autonomy from both government and academia. For example, if a particular body is to allocate research funds based on competitive applications from research universities, it must adhere strictly and transparently to a widely accepted set of procedures in soliciting and reviewing applications. It must also have full control over the resources to be allocated and have the authority and tools to sanction parties who do not abide by the established procedures.

Financing a Higher Education System

No treatment of higher education is complete without a discussion of financing, although the Task Force's treatment of this topic is not meant to be exhaustive.

In financial terms, the global higher education sector is sizeable and growing rapidly. We estimate that global spending on higher education is roughly US$300 billion, or 1 percent of global GDP, and growing at a faster pace than the world economy. Nearly one-third of this expenditure is in developing countries and, with developing country systems heavily dominated by public universities that tend to have low tuition fees, the costs fall predominantly on the state. Any attempt to improve quality will therefore add to higher education's daunting financial requirements.

Financial dependence on the state means that funding levels fluctuate with the ups and downs of government resources. This process is exaggerated by the fact that higher education is perceived as something of a luxury in most countries. Africa and Latin America in the 1980s provide clear examples of this "feast-or-famine" syndrome, with financial insecurity

---

Makerere University in Uganda

Most universities in Africa have had great difficulty in extricating themselves from an inherited model in which their role as the repository of quality education and contributor to the public good depends upon total state control and finance. This condition persisted throughout the early postindependence years of manpower planning, later experiments with developmental objectives, and the subsequent decade of demoralization and deterioration, when student numbers overwhelmed government resources. In recent years, Makerere University in Uganda has led others in addressing the pervasive problem of how to provide good-quality higher education to large numbers equitably, but without undue dependence on public resources. Restructuring at Makerere has had three central and interrelated elements: implementing alternative financing strategies, installing new management structures, and introducing demand-driven courses.

During the 1990s, Makerere moved from the brink of collapse to the point where it aspires to become again one of East Africa's pre-eminent intellectual and capacity-building resources, as it was in the 1960s. It has more than doubled student enrollment,

instigated major improvements in the physical and academic infrastructure, decentralized administration, and moved from a situation where none of its students paid fees to one where more than 70 percent do. Where previously the government covered all running costs, now more than 30 percent of revenue is internally generated. Among varied uses of this revenue, the most important is application to academic infrastructure and the retention of faculty, permitting them to devote themselves full-time to the teaching and research they were trained to do. Funds gained from nongovernment sources have been allocated, according to prescribed ratios, to library enrichment, faculty development, staff salary supplementation, and building maintenance, including some construction. The most important impact of increased institutional income has been on staff salary structures and incentive schemes. Professors can now earn over US$1,300 per month with the possibility of added supplementation on an hourly basis from evening classes. The consequence has been to slow the exodus of academic staff and remove their need to undertake a range of activities outside the university. Makerere has also introduced

---

and instability preventing long-term planning. In many Central American countries, higher education budgets are constitutionally fixed as a percentage of government spending. Although this is intended to depoliticize funding, the Task Force believes that it actually weakens the incentives for good performance, as well as creating a wide perception that higher education receives an unfair slice of the national cake. Most students come from relatively well-off backgrounds, and other vital sectors are continually forced to compete for their budgetary allotments.

In the long run, investment in higher education may be expected to promote the growth of national income, providing public funds that can, in turn, be used to finance better quality higher education. But this investment has a long gestation period, far exceeding the patience of financially strapped governments. The lack of sustainable financing therefore continues to limit enrollment growth and to skew higher education toward low-cost, low-quality programs.

The financing of higher education does not need to be limited to the public purse. In fact, higher education can be provided and financed either entirely publicly, or entirely

---

Box 4 continued

evening classes, boosted income from services like the bookshop and bakery by running them commercially, and established a consultancy bureau with staff where a portion of the generated revenue goes back into the university.

The reasons for Makerere's tradition-breaking accomplishment can be found in the interplay between a supportive external environment and an innovative institutional context. Among the most important contextual factors have been macroeconomic reform, which has led to steady economic growth and increased amounts of disposable income, and political stability, which has strengthened the government's willingness to respect university autonomy. Inside the institution, much of the reform accomplishment can be ascribed to the energy and imagination of the university's leadership, their faith in the benefits of professional, participatory, and decentralized management, their unambiguous sense of ownership of the reform process, and their commitment to a tradition of academic excellence.

The Makerere accomplishment has lessons for other universities in Africa that face similar resource constraints. It shows that expansion—and the maintenance of quality—can be achieved simultaneously in a context of reduced state funding. It puts to rest the notion that the state must be the sole provider of higher education in Africa. It dramatizes the point that a supportive political and economic environment is a prerequisite for institutional reform. It also demonstrates the variety of institutional factors involved in creating a management structure suited to ensuring the use of resources, not simply for broadening institutional offerings, but for creating the academic ethos and infrastructure on which the university's contribution to the public good depends.

Clearly, Makerere must make further progress if it is to become a world class institution. Income generation, disengagement from the state, and managerial improvement do not alone ensure academic quality. The flowering of entrepreneurial imagination, and the explosion of course offerings geared to the market, are refreshing in their relevance and departure from past patterns. However, the challenge for Makerere is to find incentives for quality research, as well as teaching, and to promote the public interest above and beyond the limits of the market.

privately (including by nongovernmental organizations), or by some combination of the two. Given that a purely public system is ill-positioned to satisfy the demands for excellence and access, and that a purely private system does not adequately safeguard the public interest, hybrid systems deserve serious consideration. The range of possibilities is depicted in Table 2.

There are both advantages and disadvantages to the provision and financing arrangements that fall into each of the three cells. Public financing and provision of higher education (cell I in Table 2) is, in many ways, the traditional paradigm for most developing countries, and is treated extensively throughout this report.

Private provision of higher education is attractive because it can lead to the delivery of more or better education at the same overall public cost. It can be coupled with public financing (cell II), as in the case of a voucher system in which the government awards funding to students who are free to enroll in different institutions (or gives the money directly to the institution after the student enrolls). In principle, this system gives universities a powerful incentive to provide quality education at a reasonable cost. However, vouchers

are not a cure-all and are ineffective when competition is weak. In many countries reliable information about competing institutions is not available and students are therefore unable to make informed decisions, while in sparsely populated (especially rural) areas there are unlikely to be enough institutions to allow student choice (although distance learning may change this to a certain extent).

Private financing is attractive because it reduces the burden on government budgets, and helps ensure that the costs of higher education are borne by those to whom the benefits accrue. Private financing (cell III) can be achieved in the context of public provision via tuition and fees, as well as grants and contracts from foundations and industry. In the case of private, not-for-profit institutions (and, in principle, public institutions as well), income from private endowment funds can also be used to support teaching and research activities.

Pakistan provides an example of a country whose higher education system has traditionally been dominated by a stifling set of public institutions and oversight bodies. Recently, however, private individuals and corporate entities have proved willing to finance and operate new philanthropic universities (cell III). This has proven beneficial both for indi-

| Table 2 | Assigning Responsibility for Higher Education |

Financing	Provision	
	Public	Private
Public	I. Free public universities and other institutions of higher education, relying on public funds to cover operating and capital expenditures.	II. Voucher systems under which the government pays a preset amount to the private schools students attend.
Private	III. Tuition, fees, and income from foundation grants, industry contracts, and privately generated endowment cover full costs.	

vidual students and for the system as a whole. The Aga Khan University (AKU) and the Lahore University of Management Sciences (LUMS) have both been established (and partly operated) through private philanthropy. In the case of the AKU, the goal of establishing a university was to improve the quality of life of disadvantaged Pakistanis through instruction and research in health sciences, education, and other fields. By contrast, LUMS was created to overcome problems of low quality in bureaucratic public universities and to help ensure a steady supply of well-trained business people.

An extraordinary level of private and international resources helped make both AKU and LUMS successful. Of course, most initiatives cannot count on such bountiful financial resources. In addition, entrenched bureaucracies can thwart even the soundest of initiatives. For example, the Bangladesh Rural Advancement Committee (BRAC), one of the developing world's most celebrated nongovernmental organizations, applied in early 1997 to Bangladesh's Ministry of Education, under the Private University Act passed in 1992, for permission to start an undergraduate institution. Financing for BRAC University was projected at a much lower level than for AKU or LUMS. Although the application was recommended for approval by the University Grants Commission, it still awaits action by the Ministry of Education, which is in the midst of working with Parliament on crafting a new national education policy. Whereas both AKU and LUMS serve as vivid proof that excellence can be achieved by private institutions that have, among other assets, adequate resources and good relations with the government, the long delays and more limited funding that characterize BRAC's experience are more typical in the developing world.

Jordan, Malaysia, and Turkey—among others—provide additional examples of institutions founded through private philanthropy.

However, business and individual philanthropy toward higher education is relatively uncommon in developing countries. Results could undoubtedly be improved through tax policy, as has been shown in Chile, where the provision of favorable tax incentives provided a powerful boost for higher education. The case of Peru provides further confirmation: university fundraising dropped sharply following the reduction of relevant tax incentives in the mid-1990s.

There is another important downside to private financing—it may preclude the enrollment of deserving students who do not have the ability to pay, and often evokes resentment among students who do. Means-tested scholarship and loan programs are one possible approach to addressing this problem, but they have proven very difficult to administer due to the difficulty of assessing ability to pay, sometimes exorbitant administrative costs, corruption, and high rates of default. The need for scholarships often provides a compelling justification for creating endowment funds, especially in philanthropic institutions, but also in public institutions.

The Task Force believes that a higher education system confined to one of the three cells shown in Table 2 is unlikely to yield desirable outcomes. The goals of a higher education system, which span quality, access, and efficiency, are surely best achieved by a diverse set of arrangements for institutional finance and service delivery. Countries need diverse systems, where some institutions look for funding from a single source while others seek a combination of public and private financing.

Multilateral and bilateral donors also have a role to play in the financing of higher education, in order to encourage the national and international public interest, as well as the contribution that higher education can make to social equity. Long-term and concessionary loans for higher education can help governments invest in higher education in a more sustained and consistent fashion, while debt relief can be negotiated in exchange for systemic higher education reform. However, the international community needs to be careful about imposing reforms from outside, and also needs to consider carefully the extent to which it can single out higher education for special treatment.

An often-neglected policy is to allow individual institutions the autonomy to develop new ways of raising revenue. Offering executive training programs, marketing the expertise of faculty, and providing various other services such as carrying out laboratory tests and renting facilities, can all provide valuable income. It is necessary to make it legally permissible to receive such funds and to use them in a discretionary manner, and also to impose limits on the extent to which proprietary research can be conducted. Centralized programs for teacher training and experiments with distance learning can also help to contain costs and improve educational quality throughout the system.

Conclusions

The new realities facing higher education (see Chapter 1) mean that many traditional ways of running higher education systems are becoming less relevant. A laissez-faire approach, which assumes that all the components of a higher education system will simply fit to-gether and serve everyone's needs, is untenable. System-wide coordination is clearly needed. But neither is centralized control the answer. Diversity is greatly needed, as are autonomy and competition among similar institutions. Funding models will also have to adapt, moving toward a flexible system that draws on both the public and the private purse.

The balance between the public and private sector is currently changing. Public higher education systems cannot meet sharp increases in demand and, as a result, the private components of higher education systems (especially for-profit institutions) have grown relatively quickly. But the growth of the private sector has tended to be quite haphazard. As a result, in most developing countries no clearly identified set of individuals or institutions is working to ensure that all the goals of the country's higher education sector will be fulfilled.

A coherent and rational approach toward management of the entire higher education sector is therefore needed. More traditional, informal arrangements are no longer adequate. Policymakers must decide on the extent to which they will guide the development of their country's higher education sector, and the extent to which they think market forces will lead to the establishment and operation of a viable system. Overall, the Task Force believes that government guidance is an essential part of any solution.

Chapter 4　Governance

The term "governance" indicates the formal and informal arrangements that allow higher education institutions to make decisions and take action. It includes external governance, which refers to relations between individual institutions and their supervisors, and internal governance, which refers to lines of authority within institutions. Governance overlaps considerably with management; the latter is seen as the implementation and execution of policies, and is dealt with primarily under "Tools for Achieving Good Governance," below.

Formal governance is official and explicit. Informal governance refers to the unwritten rules that govern how people relate to each other within higher education: the respect accorded professors and administrators, the freedom to pursue research, and the traditions of student behavior, to name a few. It is vital to articulate the rights and responsibilities of the various actors and to set rules that determine their interaction in a way that is consistent with achieving quality higher education.

The Task Force believes it is difficult to exaggerate the importance of good governance for higher education, with a significant number of those we consulted believing it to be the key issue. Good governance is not a sufficient condition for achieving high quality, but it is certainly a necessary one. Governance sets the parameters for management. A mismanaged enterprise cannot flourish, and institutions of higher education are no exception.

Although higher education has much to learn from the world's most successful businesses and government organizations, it differs significantly from these institutions. It has unique attributes developed over centuries—indeed, many of the oldest continually functioning institutions in the world are universities—and these must be carefully fostered. Higher education institutions rely on individual initiative and creativity, and these need time and space to develop. The institutional time horizon is usually much longer than in industry, with the bottom line blurred. Collegiality is a value to be cultivated, alongside considerable academic autonomy. In low- and middle-income countries, significant work is still needed to develop academic systems of governance that meet the needs of faculty, students, and wider society.

Major Principles of Good Governance

Traditions of governance differ from country to country. In some, a system-wide approach predominates over an individualistic, institutional approach. The European or continental system of higher education, for example, has been based largely on a state supervision model. As discussed in Chapter 3, some developing countries are moving from state control toward a state-supervised system, with the transition mediated by intermediary or buffer mechanisms that allow active participation by key players in higher education. Considerable differences are also apparent between public and private institutions, with Latin America diluting the European model as a growing number of private institutions challenge the role of the state within the higher education system.

Individual institutions within each country also have their own governance traditions, ranging from hierarchical to cooperative governance models. American universities, for example, use a relatively hierarchical ("unitary") style and give great power to presidents and other executives. The European tradition has weaker executives. As each institution is different, so is the way it is governed. A research university, for example, will surely have a model that is different from that of a junior college or vocational school.

Despite these many variations, the Task Force believes the following set of principles has general and lasting applicability.

Academic Freedom

Academic freedom is "the right of scholars to pursue their research, to teach, and to publish without control or restraint from the institutions that employ them" (*The Columbia Encyclopedia*). Without it, universities are unable to fulfil one of their prime functions: to be a catalyst and sanctuary for new ideas, including those that may be unpopular. Academic freedom is not an absolute concept; it has limits and requires accountability. It recognizes the right of academics to define their own areas of inquiry and to pursue the truth as they see it. Academic freedom can make a significant contribution to promoting the quality of both institutions and the system as a whole, but it needs to be understood and respected, both within institutions and by the bodies to which they are accountable.

Shared Governance

Shared governance, also known as cooperative governance, is a necessity. It arises from the concept of relative expertise and aims to ensure that decisions are devolved to those who are best qualified to make them. At the system level, it entails giving institutions or their advocates a role in shaping national higher education policy. At the institutional level, it ensures that faculty are given a meaningful voice in determining policy. This applies particularly to educational policy, and especially to curriculum development and academic appointments.

The internal governance of universities requires professionals, or rather individuals who understand how institutions can best perform their academic duties. In nearly all circumstances, individuals with advanced academic training and experience are the best choice for performing these tasks. The use of inexperienced outsiders can be, and frequently has been, damaging. This is not intended to question the legitimacy of external supervision of colleges and universities. That is external governance and is legitimately the realm of nonspecialists who represent the public will. Ultimately, however, good decisions must be rooted in legitimate professional concerns, with experience showing that shared governance is closely related to institutional quality.

The role of students within a system of shared governance can be controversial. Students are a transient population whose stay at educational institutions lasts only a few years, while faculty members and administrators tend to remain at institutions for long periods of time. Faculty and administrators therefore have natural authority over students in many matters of internal governance, particularly with respect to academic matters such as admissions standards, grading policy, and degree requirements.

Students, however, can play a role in areas that affect their lives and in which they have competence to provide constructive input. In nonacademic areas, this would include extracurricular activities, and the administration of housing and student services. In academic areas, too, there is an appropriate role for student input, including in the areas of program offerings, teacher evaluation, and infrastructure requirements.

Clear Rights and Responsibilities

Mutually agreed rights and responsibilities for each element in the higher education system are essential for good governance. Externally, the roles of ministries of education and higher education institutions must be clearly articulated by law and in national policy documents. Internally, the faculty, students, administrators, external supervisors, and others should have a clear understanding of their rights and responsibilities. Where traditions of higher education are new, as in many developing countries, it is especially important that roles are explicit, through clear laws and institutional charters designed as social contracts.

Meritocratic Selection

Higher education can only function if the selection and promotion of faculty, administrators, and students is based on broadly defined merit. The particular goals of an institution may affect how it assesses merit, but ideology, nepotism, cronyism, or intimidation cannot be allowed to determine advancement. Selection decisions must be autonomous, made within the institution by those closest to the issues, with peer review and wide consultation helping to set appropriate merit standards. Decisionmaking by distant bureaucrats or politicians is not to be encouraged, with legal barriers that prevent the recognition of merit

being especially unhelpful. In Venezuela and some other countries, for example, a raise for one faculty member in one institution leads, by law, to the same raise for all faculty members of equal rank in all institutions. In some instances, fortunately infrequent, professors are the greatest barriers to progress and change in these matters. If that happens, the governing authorities must ensure the presence of strong internal leadership that can push through change.

Financial Stability

Higher education institutions require sufficient financial stability to permit orderly development. Financial uncertainty, sharp budgetary fluctuations, and political favoritism hinder good governance and make rational planning impossible. The importance of higher education as a public good must be matched by adequate public investment to enable institutions to discharge their public responsibilities.

The provider of financing can also undermine autonomy, with major sponsors trying to influence the activities of higher education institutions. This is a particular danger in developing countries, where a single institution such as the state or a religious entity tends to contribute a relatively large share of the resources available to higher education institutions.

Accountability

Higher education institutions must be accountable to their sponsors, whether public or private. Accountability does not imply uncontrolled interference, but it does impose a requirement to periodically explain actions and have successes and failures examined in a transparent fashion. All interaction should occur within the context of agreed rights and responsibilities. Buffer mechanisms, as already discussed, may be needed to help determine the appropriate balance between autonomy and accountability.

Regular Testing of Standards

Those responsible for governance should regularly test and verify standards of quality. This is part of institutional accountability, but is of sufficient importance to list as a separate principle. Broad consultation should be practiced and standards should be widely agreed upon. Benchmarking is useful in this regard, while peer review encourages the attainment of benchmarks.

The Importance of Close Cooperation

Effective governance requires close cooperation and compatibility between different levels of institutional administration. A useful rule would state that for significant appointments the individual in a supervisory position, for example a dean, has a formal role—more than merely a voice—in selecting the appointee, for example a chairperson. This could prevent counterproductive, adversarial situations, a special problem where the tradition of election prevails.

The Actual Situation

Systems of governance must take institutional goals into account, and not all principles apply with equal force to all institutions of higher education. In research universities, the full set is most important, whereas academic freedom or shared governance may be less important in vocational schools. For-profit, private education—as noted above, a rapidly growing sector—presents special problems. These businesses are responsible to investors seeking financial gains, but must also accommodate these principles within their business model if they are to play their part in the wider higher education system.

Despite these variations, it is abundantly clear that these principles are essential, and also equally clear that they are routinely violated across the world, in rich and poor countries alike. They are probably violated with greater frequency in developing countries, as in these four examples:

- A senior observer of the African scene told the Task Force that "with the government in many countries having assumed the power to appoint and dismiss the Vice-Chancellor, governance in the universities has thus become a purely state-controlled system . . . There are countries where even deans and department heads are also appointed by government and where heads of institutions change with a change in government."

- In China, the presidents of two leading universities, Beijing and Tsinghua, are appointed directly by the State Council, comprising the Prime Minister and the Cabinet, acting upon the recommendation of the Communist Party.

- The Civic Education Project, a US-based, nongovernmental organization operating in parts of the former Soviet Union, commented to the Task Force "hiring practices in universities are *ad hoc* and personnel are under the influence of high officials in the president's office or the Ministries of Education. Higher administrative authorities can hire or fire any staff or teacher as and when they wish. Teachers have hardly any voice and influence in reforming the higher education system. Students are rarely considered as part of the higher education administrative process. They are never consulted on any matter related to their education. Decisions are made from the top and imposed on the subordinate bodies. There is no public debate or discussion on the reform of higher education. Even in the most reform-minded central Asian states, the press and media are controlled by governments and there is no open social dialogue or debate on reform in such a crucial sector of national life as higher education."

- Between the early 1980s and 1996, the total number of higher education institutions in El Salvador increased from six to 42. Many of these were low-quality, "garage" universities, resulting from poor external governance. Despite a law calling for close regulation of universities by the Ministry of Education, supervision was in practice quite lax, with institutions not required to demonstrate their competency to provide education.

These examples are typical and point to poor governance as a particular obstacle to the improvement of quality in the developing world.

Why Governance is a Special Problem in Developing Countries

Higher education institutions inevitably reflect the societies in which they operate. When a country suffers from deep rifts, these will be present on the campus. Undemocratic countries are unlikely to encourage shared governance in higher education. A society in which corruption is prevalent cannot expect its higher education institutions to be untainted. In other words, external factors easily overwhelm institutional efforts to promote change and are, of course, especially difficult to change.

For many of the countries in the developing world, political leaders at the start of independence exhibited little understanding and sometimes little sympathy for the needs

of university education. However, at independence and still today, most problems faced by developing countries were believed to require some degree of government guidance and supervision. Higher education was no exception, leading to policymakers, with little sympathy to its needs, managing it in the same way they managed roads, the army, or customs. The failure to recognize the importance of taking the long-term view undermined the higher education sector's performance and inhibited the development of governance traditions. The proliferation of new institutions in most developing countries has now diluted whatever useful traditions existed and also created shortages of qualified personnel.

The tendency of politicians to intervene in higher education left many institutions hostage to factional policies, with decisions on student selection, faculty appointments and promotions, curriculum design, and similar matters being made on political grounds rather than on merit. In addition, many country leaders undoubtedly saw universities as sources of political danger, with students playing a relatively active political role. Governments may fear students because they know that these young people could, under certain circumstances, overthrow a regime. Therefore many governments expect universities to contain student political activism, further corrupting the governance systems within institutions.

Simultaneously, political activism means that students are spending a large proportion of their time on politics rather than on education. The Task Force believes strongly that higher education institutions should allow opinions on the broader issues that face society to be expressed and debated respectfully. Student awareness and debate should therefore be encouraged. There are situations, however, where levels of activism can rise to the point where high-quality education becomes impossible. In Africa and elsewhere, students facing the prospect of underemployment or unemployment upon graduation have demonstrated during examinations to prolong their stay in school. In situations such as these, where academic pursuits have been taken hostage, activism may need to be restricted.

In conclusion, there are clearly many obstacles in the path of achieving good governance within the higher education systems of developing countries. Despite this, there are also many tools for achieving improvement.

Tools for Achieving Good Governance

The term "governance" refers to a large set of specific policies and practices. The Task Force does not offer an exhaustive treatment of governance and managerial tools, but attempts to demonstrate available options and their respective advantages and disadvantages.

At the system level, the first priority is to reach agreement on the nature of the governance model to be used. At an institutional level, there should be clarity over the legal framework, and an understanding of the principles of central governance. Decisions can then be made, at both the system and institutional levels, as to the best mechanisms or tools to make the proposed model work effectively.

Faculty Councils (or Senates)

Faculty councils are representative bodies of faculty members responsible for making decisions about selected matters of academic policy, such as programs offered, curricula, degree requirements, and admissions policy. Delegating powers to a faculty council (or senate) promotes shared governance by limiting the extent to which higher education institutions are run on a top-down basis.

Governing Councils (or Boards of Trustees)

A governing council is an independent body that acts as a buffer between a higher education institution and the external bodies to which the institution is accountable, such as the state and religious or secular sponsors. These bodies represent the institution to the outside world, and at the same time represent the outside world to the institution. Critically, they help insulate higher education institutions from excessive external interference.

A governing council needs to think about the future, and it will often be involved in developing long-term plans for an institution and monitoring their implementation. Appointments to the council need to be for long periods, allowing council members to act independently and remain insulated from short-term political developments. Membership should be mixed, with a significant number of members drawn from outside the academic community.

Similar bodies can be tied to subject areas, rather than institutions. National foundations for the natural sciences, the social sciences, and the humanities can sit between the government and the university sector. Their independence allows them to implement merit-based procedures for resource allocation that are relatively immune to political influence.

Budget Practices and Financial Management

Creating a transparent, logical, and well-understood set of rules for budgeting and accounting can have an enormous influence on the operation and performance of higher education institutions. Rules should encourage flexibility, stability, and transparency. In many institutions across the world, bureaucratic rigidity results in inefficiency and waste. Allowing the flexibility, for example, for institutions to carry surpluses from one year to the next, or to transfer funds from one budgetary category to another, may counter the "use-it-or-lose-it" attitude referred to in Chapter 1 and lead to a better planned allocation of limited funds. Stability is increased by setting multiyear budgets, allowing higher education institutions to extend their planning horizons and expand their set of feasible options. Flexibility helps promote stability when financial rules allow institutions to accumulate capital assets from private sources, and to build endowments whose annual income can be projected far into the future. Transparency, finally, is at the heart of budgeting and financial management and is especially important in situations where corruption is undermining the higher education sector.

Data for Decisionmaking

Without good data, effective decisionmaking is impossible. Higher education institutions need a plethora of data on teaching and research performance, student achievement, institutional financial status, and so on. Data are also essential for systems of monitoring and accountability, which allow institutional autonomy while promoting competition and the drive for higher standards.

Higher education needs to take advantage of advances in information technology, which greatly facilitate data collection and analysis. With good data, organized in a readily accessible information system, higher education institutions will be able to improve their policymaking, ensuring that decisions are based on evidence and are made in a way that is clear and understandable to the outside world.

Appointment or Election?

Election of academic leaders is common in many universities across the world, although it often results in weak leadership and a consequent prejudice in favor of the status quo. Appointed leaders, meanwhile, are less likely to allow their programs to be stalled by lack of consensus and are better placed to make unpopular decisions when required. However, they can lack widespread support, diluting a sense of shared governance. In-depth consultation with all stakeholders helps ease this problem and increases the appointed leader's legitimacy.

The Task Force believes that universities in the developing world urgently need strong leadership, whatever selection method is employed. On the whole, it is in favor of strengthening appointing powers within university administrations, in order to allow strong leaders to emerge.

Faculty Appointment and Promotion Decisions

Faculty quality is generally accepted as the most important determinant of the overall quality of a higher education institution. Nepotism, cronyism, and inbreeding are powerful enemies of faculty quality. The practice of rewarding length of service, rather than academic performance and promise, is also to be discouraged.

The Task Force wishes to emphasize the importance of external peer review in making appointments to faculty and deciding on promotion. Evaluation of faculty research by qualified outsiders allows its quality to be judged on proper technical grounds. Assessments are also more likely to be free of conflicts of interest. Peer review also promotes the quality of publication decisions and the efficient allocation of research funds.

The system of peer review has been developed within research universities. Functional equivalents need to be developed for institutions with different missions. Institutions must develop clear indicators to assess the quality of their organizational objectives. For example, faculties can be systematically evaluated on their success in teaching or imparting vocational skills. Regular inspections by "client" representatives can also prove useful.

Security of Employment

Security of employment is important within higher education institutions. It allows faculty members greater academic freedom than they would have if they could be dismissed at will or were hired on a year-to-year basis. It also acts as a form of nonwage compensation, with talented individuals attracted to secure jobs, even when they could earn more lucrative salaries elsewhere.

The Task Force recommends long-term contracts, though not necessarily indefinite ones. Periodic reviews are also important, allowing faculty members to be discharged if their performance is substandard.

In some circumstances, however, faculty appointments without any time limit may be appropriate. This system, commonly known as tenure, has advantages and disadvantages. Tenure has been criticized on the grounds that it undermines the performance incentives of tenured faculty, whose appointments are rarely revoked, and even then only in cases of gross neglect, incapacity, morally reprehensible behavior, or urgent financial circumstances. By contrast, tenure is defended as being a great promoter of academic freedom, allowing faculty to pursue potentially risky and unpopular lines of research, without fear of job loss. Its proponents also argue that tenure and prestige are nonpecuniary employment conditions that allow higher education institutions to compete effectively for the services of the brightest, most creative, and most highly motivated members of society.

Tenure has a place in highly politicized environments, where finite-term contracts could be subject to abuse by key institutional decisionmakers. It can also strengthen the capacity and potential of research universities, with their more speculative and uncertain process of basic knowledge generation. Decisions about tenure must be taken with particular care. Extensive, independent, and external evidence of scholarly achievement and promise is needed, with assessments carried out by those with the technical skills that qualify them to make such judgments.

Faculty Compensation and Responsibilities

Many faculty members have specialized skills that are valued in the job market. This allows them to engage in remunerative professional activities outside their home institutions in order to supplement typically low salaries. In other cases, for example in Latin America, faculty members are forced to seek part-time appointments at several institutions, as full-time appointments are not available.

Outside work can promote professional development by providing inspiration for new research and better teaching materials. It also helps institutions to develop valuable contacts with the private sector that may lead to job opportunities for students or the opportunity for public/private collaborations. There is a downside, however. Outside activities can easily detract from performance and weaken commitment to an institution. Academic staff become less available to students, colleagues, and administrators, and the institutional culture is damaged. Faculty moonlighting is therefore rightly regarded as one of the more serious problems faced by higher education in developing countries.

Tackling this issue usually means raising pay, and nearly all developing countries will need to improve compensation if they are to achieve greater quality in their higher education systems. Moving to a system of full-time appointments may also be useful, combined with clear limits on outside activity: for example, no more than one day of outside activity (paid or unpaid) per week, with prior approval required. Institutions need to be careful when imposing limits on outside consultancy, however. If pay levels are low, they risk driving away the more able members of their faculty.

Faculty quality is also greatly threatened when compensation is determined by rigid formulas that fail to account for external labor market opportunities—a problem that is common in professional schools and institutes of technology. Salary systems must be flexible across disciplines: the market for talent has to be taken into account.

Visiting Committees and Accreditation

Visiting committees, consisting of recognized national or international experts, can be an important tool for monitoring institutional performance and promoting the responsible exercise of authority. By conducting independent reviews, visiting committees provide objective assessments of the achievements of faculties or academic programs in relation to an appropriate regional, national, or international standard. The cost of visiting committees can be prohibitive for many institutions, and it may be valuable for the public sector to subsidize these visitations for all types of schools—including for-profit schools—so as to encourage higher standards throughout the system. Even if only a few of the upper-tier institutions use visiting committees, the effects can be felt throughout the whole system if there are strong links and open competition between institutions.

International standards of accreditation—for example, those used by external examiners—also promote institutional quality. Internally, they provide a focus for improving standards and help create a sense of institutional pride. Externally, they provide the market information that is vital to competition. Being accredited has great value in attracting students, faculty, and other resources.

El Salvador provides a notable example of the power of accreditation. In December 1995, the government started to tackle the proliferation of low-quality universities by establishing a new system of accreditation. Institutions that did not satisfy specific statutory requirements within 24 months were subject to closure, and the authorities had actually closed 11 institutions by early 1998 (with a program for relocating the displaced students). With the cooperation of Salvadoran universities, the Ministry of Education also established a system of self-study and peer review, including the training of 120 volunteer peer reviewers. The Task Force applauds this kind of system, which generates objective information that the public can use to judge the merits of competing higher education institutions.

Institutional Charters and Handbooks

An institutional charter establishes the legal basis and defines the mission of a higher education institution. It also sets forth rules governing its relations with the state or a private sponsor, and may specify some internal rules of operation as well. It centers the institution and sets the tone for all of its other activities.

Faculty and student handbooks can be an important tool for promoting good internal governance. They must be comprehensive, clearly written, and frequently updated. Faculty handbooks should typically include a general statement of faculty rights and responsibilities, along with detailed information to guide the conduct of faculty members with respect to their teaching and research activities, their participation in the broader life of the institution, and their outside professional activities. Student handbooks generally define the objectives, rules, and requirements of different academic programs, as well as students' nonacademic rights and responsibilities.

Conclusions

Good governance promotes educational quality. Traditions of governance vary from country to country and by type of institution, but the Task Force has suggested a set of basic principles that promote good governance across a wide variety of situations. Unfortunately these principles are frequently not observed, especially in developing countries, and especially where traditions of higher education are still not firmly established. The Task Force has therefore offered a number of tools that will help higher education systems and institutions move closer to the application of these principles.

Good governance may be crucial, but it is not a panacea. In many parts of the world, pedagogy takes the form of canned lectures by professors and rote memorization by students; cheating is rampant and tolerated; and letters of recommendation are for sale. Shared governance does not guarantee quality if a tyrannical majority is determined to prevent progress. Perhaps most importantly, quality is not likely to be achieved as long as professors are forced to moonlight as a consequence of inadequate pay.

The Task Force hopes that higher education policymakers will start to make better use of the tools of good governance. They will not solve all problems quickly. But they will start the process of achieving sustainable and far-reaching improvement.

Chapter 5 Science and Technology

Science education, in the broad sense…is a fundamental prerequisite for democracy and for ensuring sustainable development.

Declaration on Science and the Use of Scientific Knowledge,
World Conference on Science, Budapest, 2 July 1999

A Worldwide Issue

Science and technology advances are transforming the world at an astonishing rate. Developments in computing and communications, in particular, are helping to accelerate these changes. Organizations in even the most advanced economies struggle to keep up, while developing countries face serious threats, as well as some new opportunities.

The recent World Conference on Science—the first such conference in 20 years—took place as the Task Force was drafting this report. The Task Force warmly welcomes both the Declaration on Science and the Use of Scientific Knowledge and the accompanying Framework for Action, which reflects and deepens many of the themes outlined below. In particular, we embrace the framework's clear and unambiguous call that "governments should accord the highest priority to improving science education at all levels" and should work closely in this endeavor with the private sector and civil society.

Our emphasis is narrower than that of the Conference: higher education is, we believe, an absolute and irreducible prerequisite to developing a strong science and technology base. We balance this interest in science with a call for increased priority for general education (Chapter 6). Tomorrow's world will

demand highly qualified specialists and increasingly flexible generalists. Higher education needs to be ready to meet both these demands.

Background

The North–South scientific gap is large and growing—in part due to the very nature of scientific and technological advances in the computing age. Further research will be required to quantify the extent of the gap, but there is enough evidence to show that it is huge.

For example, on a *per capita* basis developed countries have nearly ten times as many research and development scientists and technicians as developing countries (3.8 versus 0.4 per 1,000). They have a much higher share of their populations studying science at the tertiary level, principally due to substantially greater enrollment rates. Further, they are spending some 2 percent of GDP on R&D, compared to a rate of 0.5 percent or less in most developing countries. Western Europe, North America, Japan, and the newly industrialized East Asian countries account for 84 percent of scientific articles published. These regions also provide more than 97 percent of all new patents registered in Europe and the United States.

Science and technology have direct impacts on society (Box 5)—and such impacts can translate directly into economic growth. A well-developed higher education sector is fundamental here: it allows countries to generate new scientific knowledge, to wisely select and implement existing technologies, and to effectively adapt them to local circumstances. To achieve these tasks, higher education science and technology badly needs more investment and more efficient allocation of existing resources. This will require a formidable effort.

The North–South scientific gap is characterized by stark differences in:

- access to high-quality laboratory facilities, equipment, and supplies;

- the availability of well-trained teachers;

- the proportion of well-prepared and motivated students;

- links with the international scientific community; and

- access to the global stock of up-to-date knowledge.

Box 5

A Double-Edged Sword

Science and technology have a good track record in generating and applying new knowledge to improve the human condition. They can justly claim to have made a positive difference to the lives of billions. High-yielding varieties of rice, sulfa drugs, powerful antibiotics, oral contraceptives, electricity, and cheap and durable plastics are just a few examples of scientific advances that have had an enormous, direct, and positive impact on living standards across the world.

Not only is the practice of science and technology important to development, but so are its intrinsic values. These values generate, in turn, positive spillovers for the wider task of modernization and social transformation as the creativity, objectivity, and healthy skepticism about both old and new claims that are important to science find a wider application. And it is in higher education institutions that many of these values are championed. However, scientific and technological "progress" can also threaten the public interest. Nuclear missiles posed an extreme threat to world security for decades, but with the Cold War over, developing countries are now diverting scarce resources into developing their own nuclear capacity. Advances in genetics bring a host of moral and practical problems. Private industry is currently patenting new ways of producing food at an astonishing rate. Terminator genes, which are used solely for the purpose of rendering sterile new, high-yielding seeds, are one example of a technology that appears to be in the interest of industry rather than farmers. Monsanto's recent announcement that it would not pursue their commercial use was a response to both US farmers' concerns and a campaign by, and on behalf of, developing-world farmers.

But even these problems are exacerbated by a lack of indigenous science capacity in developing countries. Foreign experts can catalyze and contribute to various initiatives, but they cannot provide the sustained input that is needed to help developing countries use science as a tool for development rather than destruction.

Science and technology have, to some extent, the character of a public good—and market forces often provide less demand for scientific research than is socially desirable. National governments (both singly and in concert) must therefore act to counter this market failure. International organizations must play a vital role, recognizing the global public benefits of scientific inquiry and education. National and international organizations have the ability to finance large investments in the development and maintenance of scientific capacity—and to support long-term efforts in science when exact benefits are often difficult to predict. National and international organizations also have a duty to increase the public understanding of science, encouraging public support for the values embodied in scientific inquiry.

The Task Force recommends the following five areas for specific action:

- physical and technical resources;

- human resources;

- local, regional, and international cooperation;

- strategies for scientific development; and

- university–industry cooperation.

Physical and Technical Resources

By their very nature, science and technology have always demanded significant, ongoing investment to establish, maintain, and expand the "engine" of physical infrastructure—including laboratories, libraries, and classrooms. They also need a rich (and expensive) fuel of textbooks, computers, equipment, and other supplies. Investment in physical capital is often prohibitively expensive, with tariffs on imported goods, particularly computer hard-

ware and software, contributing to the problem. India's formidable software industry, for example, did not develop until the removal of high tariffs on imported computers. Had these barriers fallen sooner, India might well have enjoyed the economic benefits of this rapidly growing sector much earlier. The Task Force believes it to be especially important that governments consider tariff exemptions for scientific and technical equipment imported by educational institutions.

Developing countries could also benefit to a much greater extent from the second-hand, but essentially state-of-the-art, research instrumentation that can be purchased on the world market; while the equipment is currently available, many countries are not aware of it. Donor institutions should consider establishing a not-for-profit global clearinghouse for this equipment. It would be useful not only in higher education, but also in many developing-country industries. But shortages of scientific equipment are unlikely to be totally resolved by these measures alone. Within limits, greater government initiatives either to purchase such equipment or to engage donors in providing it would be worthwhile.

The price of appropriate textbooks is also a problem. Books are often extremely expensive in developing countries, even relative to the incomes of upper-middle-class students, and, without sufficient books, the access of university teachers and students to the world stock of knowledge is limited. International agencies already buy (or subsidize) and distribute textbooks, but they should also consider alternative solutions. In many fields, it should be possible for instructors at different institutions to achieve some degree of coordination in their adoption of a relatively small set of textbooks. Such coordination narrows the range of perspectives to which students are exposed, but it allows bulk buying of books that greatly reduces costs. This policy could be combined with the relocating of production to developing countries. With regional cooperation, the production of a single Asian edition of a key textbook would be possible, for example using lower-cost local publishing houses. Successful examples of this policy already exist in other fields, for example in health, where the bulk purchase of pharmaceuticals is common. Higher education institutions should also make more extensive use of editions of books published within the past year or two, which are often available at significant discounts.

Computer-based technologies have the potential to dramatically transform higher education in developing countries, and are clearly applicable to science education. Networks and new forms of teaching media have already influenced training and research in industrial countries. They reduce intellectual isolation while providing increased (and ever-faster) access to the very latest scientific information—serving as "learning commons" (see Chapter 3). The research capabilities of the Internet, combined with basic word-processing software, can increase the ability of researchers to contribute to mainstream scientific publications. Intelligent tutoring systems and instructional software offer uniformly high-quality training on complex topics. Some of this technology is supplied in novel and flexible ways. Internet cafés are springing up in all corners of the world, providing reliable and relatively low-cost access to the Internet. Others must be provided centrally—and require substantial ongoing investment.

Another sector experiencing technology-driven change is distance learning (see Chapter 1), which will continue to grow as education reinvents itself in the digital age. However, science and technology education frequently depends on direct, hands-on experience of complex experimental techniques and technologies. As yet these are difficult to deliver via the Internet. Further, it is through a period of time spent in tertiary education insti-

tutions that almost all seriously able scientists and technicians enter the marketplace. And while corporate education initiatives continue to develop, more traditional modes of higher education will continue to have a vital role to play in skillfully developing the interest, initiative, and knowledge base of science and technology students at a critical stage in their lives.

Computers and Internet connections are available in nearly all developing countries, and access will increase sharply as computer costs continue to decline, and wireless communications systems and solar-powered electric generators proliferate in remote locations. In the meantime, many countries use outdated computers that cannot run the latest versions of many programs. Unless computer equipment can be updated frequently, both students and scientists will be frustrated in their efforts to keep pace with scientific developments in the industrial world. The pace of technological change in the industrial countries is so fast that some such frustration is almost inevitable—but for countries and institutions where computers are still extremely scarce, older computers, available at low cost, will be quite valuable. The key to this is to understand the limits of older software and hardware. Older technology is never a panacea when the pace of change is so rapid. If educational institutions can convince people (and local small businesses in particular) of the fact that older computers are often perfectly adequate for many tasks, they will be better placed to sell off such equipment in order to invest in newer models. Further, the notion of global clearing-houses for research instrumentation outlined above is equally applicable to computing technology. Similarly, the many imaginative schemes developed by several sectors to provide, for example, agricultural tools, spectacles, pharmaceuticals, and books for the developing world could also be extended to computing power.

Human Resources

Scientists working in developing countries have certainly made contributions to the world's stock of scientific knowledge and technological know-how. The contribution made by Chinese traditional medicines to healthcare has been significant, spanning from acupuncture to treatments for a form of leukemia. However, a far greater number of developing-country scientists have contributed only minimally, often from want of adequate training, facilities, supplies, access to scientific literature, and interaction with knowledgeable and imaginative colleagues.

The lack of well-qualified science and technology teachers and researchers is a widespread problem in developing countries, particularly in Africa, with its very small base of individuals who can create a science-oriented culture (although see Box 7, below).

Faculty salaries and benefits therefore need urgent attention. It is also clear that industry has a significant role to play in the area of science and technology. The knowledge society is encouraging a much closer relationship between governments, researchers, and commercial interests, with new alliances increasingly recognized. Governments are frequently directing research aims toward the good of the national economy, while industry looks for quick commercial development of academic research. Within this context, industry can play a key role in revamping incentive structures for educational institutions, imposing specific hiring standards, and establishing competitive scholarships, loans, work-study, internship, and research grant programs. Such arrangements can benefit all concerned: business, educational institutions, and students.

Brain Drain

Outstanding scientists are often peripatetic—they seek imaginative colleagues, excellent facilities and, increasingly, financial rewards. This is a problem that applies to all countries, but in developing countries, which have so few scientists, the impact of such migration can be enormous (see Box 6). Estimates indicate that about one-third of foreign students studying in the United States do not return to their home countries. Those who do return frequently bring considerable knowledge and skills back with them. There is a drawback, however, since their new expertise may well be skewed toward the research agenda of industrialized countries rather than their own.

Another, less widely noted aspect of the brain drain is known as the "camp-follower" phenomenon. Scientists and other academics in developing countries often orient their efforts toward those that are taking place in industrial countries, for example choosing topics and methods that mimic academics in other regions in order to become (or remain) part of mainstream research. When the focus abroad changes, local researchers also change their focus. The goal is often to win a temporary or permanent position abroad or to secure international funding for in-country work. The intermediate result is that, effectively, "brain drain" can take place in the absence of actual emigration.

The widespread outflow of qualified individuals stems from dissatisfaction with local conditions and inadequate scientific support—and from greater intellectual and earning opportunities abroad. Although the new information technologies may dampen scientists' and engineers' incentives to emigrate, the brain drain phenomenon is likely to continue in the absence of specific countervailing actions. The retention of top-level talent in developing countries requires improved governance in higher education institutions, greater intellectual opportunities, higher professional salaries, and better working conditions. Countries must also develop further incentives, such as academic freedom, support

Box 6

When Students Study Overseas

In many countries, both developing and developed, significant numbers of students study at overseas institutions. (The appendix to this report gives UNESCO's figures on this phenomenon.) The benefits from this practice can be substantial as students are exposed to ideas, techniques, and entire fields of study that differ from what is on offer at home. And in many instances the quality of the education they receive is better than what is available in their own country. Not only students, but countries as a whole, can benefit from such study.

Nevertheless, a country whose students go abroad for higher education faces some disturbing consequences. First, the cost of overseas instruction, particularly if it takes place in a developed country, is generally extremely high. If the student's home country pays for this education for a large number of students, this can represent a significant fiscal drain. Even if an outside donor is paying for the student's education, study abroad means that funds from donor agencies are being used to pay for a very expensive type of higher education. Such funds could, in principle, be used more effectively to pro-

mote quality higher education in the developing country itself.

Second, study abroad is often a student's first step toward resettling abroad. A country may invest large amounts of money in training students abroad only to find that they very often do not come back. Thus, even if a student's family is paying directly for the overseas education, there is a potential negative consequence for the sending country. Various schemes have been employed to encourage students to return, but in the end they have met with only partial success. It is apparent that the benefits of this accrue with donor countries, not developing countries.

The status that accompanies overseas study, along with the skills that students learn abroad, mean that this practice will undoubtedly continue to play a prominent role in providing tertiary education to a substantial number of students from developing countries. However, given the consequences of an indefinite continuation of this tradition, countries would benefit by sufficiently improving their higher education systems to attract a greater portion of their students to study in-country.

for international collaboration, and enhanced job security, in order to lure back and retain their most talented scientists and engineers. Sustained imaginative efforts to attract and host international academic and research conferences, for example, would help contribute to the cultural revaluation of science and technology. Exchange schemes, mentor programs, and other innovative approaches could be developed to attract higher caliber researchers to the country. Scholarship and loan opportunities, targeting students who prove that they will return home following studies abroad, may also be a feasible and economically appropriate way to reduce brain drain.

India is a country that has had some success in reducing brain drain. The near-universal emigration of their computer science graduates a decade ago has now declined to 70 percent. This has largely been due to the growing number of highly paid jobs with national and multinational corporations that were established following market liberalization. Growing demand for skilled graduates in fields such as software engineering, financial services, and telecommunications has also provided some impetus for improved training in these fields.

Complex relationships are at work here, with government, industry, and academia all

African Science Moves Forward

African science recently received a boost when a particularly imaginative proposal—to explore how resources freed by debt relief can be committed to science and technology—was offered by 50 African ministers who met at the World Science Conference in Budapest. This was the largest meeting of African science ministers in more than 20 years. Cameroon's Minister of Science and Technology (and mathematician) Henri Hogbe Nlend said the conference "has given us an opportunity to relaunch inter-African cooperation in science."

The African ministers will follow the conference with another meeting, held by the Organization of African States, to discuss a pan-African scientific collaboration protocol. They hope such a protocol will be signed by heads of state. In particular, they want to explore building links between richer and poorer African countries as well as between industrialized and developing countries.

The Task Force hopes these initiatives will build on existing ones, such as The University Science, Humanities and Engineering Partnerships in Africa (USHEPiA). This is a collaborative program, launched in 1994, building on existing potential to develop a network of African researchers capable of addressing the developmental requirements of Sub-Saharan Africa. Involving universities in Botswana, Kenya, South Africa, Tanzania, Uganda, Zambia, and Zimbabwe, USHEPiA initiates fruitful educational exchanges involving masters and doctoral students, lecturers, and postdoctoral fellows. USHEPiA also promotes productive, collaborative research on problems challenging Africa.

The Task Force applauds these initiatives and hopes they will be fully developed over the coming years.

---

having a role to play. Fragmented effort will not suffice. Environment, tourism, and business development are all areas where governments have begun to recognize a need to think and act strategically across departmental interests. Science and technology increasingly define our future. It is therefore vital to the future of developing countries that they turn to the task of systematically nurturing—and retaining—their science and technology talent.

Women in Science and Technology

Although there has been measurable progress over the past 30 years, a global pattern whereby women are under-represented in all sectors of education persists; this pattern does mask important regional and local variations,

however. The widest gap by gender is seen in South Asia, the Middle East and Sub-Saharan Africa, but women are increasingly well represented in Latin America.[8] The gender imbalance is particularly strong in the areas of mathematics, the physical sciences, and engineering, but in many developing countries, this imbalance is notably smaller in the medical sciences. Women are also disproportionately enrolled in alternative forms of higher education, such as distance education, teacher training colleges, nursing schools, and nonuniversity, tertiary-level institutions. There are also clearly social pressures on women to pursue traditionally "female" subjects in the

---

[8] World Bank, *World Development Indicators 1997*, p. 73.

humanities, education, and nursing at the expense of science and technology disciplines.

As noted, this problem is by no means confined to developing countries. Approximately 2 percent of the people on the United Kingdom Engineering Council database, for example, are female. There are also many social constraints to female participation in higher education in general, with higher education perceived as a predominantly male environment. The lack of female participation in mainstream higher education and science and technology disciplines means that many countries currently realize only a portion of their potential in these areas.

Developing countries should therefore urgently explore ways to promote the participation of women in the sciences. The international development community has come to recognize the great social benefits of educating girls at the primary and secondary levels. Now it must recognize the value of educating women at the tertiary level, including in scientific fields. Once initiated, the process will gain momentum as successful female professionals—including scientists—provide positive role models. A positive result would be a narrowing of the gender gap in science and technology and a simultaneous enhancing of national scientific achievement. In addition, since professional women tend to be less internationally mobile than men, increasing the share of investment in science education directed toward women will presumably help to reduce brain drain.

Because of numerous social and cultural barriers, including falling behind their male peers when they have children, special measures may be required to help women achieve leadership roles in science. Mentoring programs for women in mathematics and science have had a positive effect on retention rates. Increasing scholarship assistance and loans to women would undoubtedly help. Actively recruiting women for graduate study and developing supportive networks (see Box 8) would also help promote a culture of female participation in science and technology.

Box 8

Gender Agenda

Women's role in science has come under increased scrutiny of late, and this was formalized when the final documentation emerging from the World Science Conference in Budapest systematically acknowledged gender issues. Sjamsiah Achmad of the Indonesian Institute of Technology in Jakarta, who chaired the gender issues session, noted "it's the first time the issue has entered the world science agenda."

Another Indonesian delegate, Wati Hermawati, welcomed the call to develop gender indicators. She will work at the National Focal Point for Gender, Science and Technology (part of Achmad's Institute) to develop gender indicators on, for example, participation, education, and career structures. "Until now we've had no indicators," she pointed out. OECD (Organization for Economic Cooperation and Development) members have carried out comparative studies of scientific efforts, but hitherto have not collected gender data. Meanwhile, UNESCO recently announced its intention to fund a science and technology network for Arab women. Another group is currently negotiating a support network in Jakarta to serve the Indonesian and Pacific region.

Improving Primary and Secondary Preparation

Recent international evidence reveals considerable cross-country variation in mathematics and scientific achievement at primary and secondary levels, both among developing and industrial countries.[9] Science and mathematics are both "building block" subjects in that progress is particularly reliant on what has already been learned. Country authorities therefore need to improve primary and secondary institutions' curriculum development, teachers' qualifications, teaching techniques, and access to key inputs such as textbooks, laboratory facilities, and information technology. Further, systematic attention at the primary and secondary levels to many of the cultural issues regarding gender would also facilitate an enhanced flow of women's participation.

Local, Regional, and International Cooperation

Higher education institutions benefit greatly from connections with similar institutions. For scientists in the developing world, the paucity of such contacts is often an impediment to their creativity and productivity. They lack a direct pipeline into current scientific awareness, lack opportunities for mainstream publication, and are part of few professional partnerships or networks. (Few things are more disconcerting to researchers than to be informed that their new "discoveries" were already known to others.) Unlike colleagues in the humanities or social sciences, much of their subject matter is almost totally incomprehensible to the wider population and it is thus even more important that developing-world scientists be able to plug into those sources of support and inspiration that do exist.

Ways of overcoming isolation include organizing conferences, providing travel grants allowing researchers to reach more distant venues, and ensuring access to telephones and computer-mediated communication. All of these actions would help promote interaction among a corps of geographically dispersed scientists. Links could also be promoted, for example, by the formation of an international volunteer corps of scientists (some of whom might be retired) who could offer their services by teaching or consulting in specific fields or on particular projects. Such pro bono cooperation, for which successful examples exist in fields such as financial service, has to be handled with care (for example, would-be helpers sometimes arrive unprepared), but the potential benefits are enormous. The Financial Services Volunteer Corps draws on working professionals in the banking and corporate sector and since 1990 has sent over 1,000 volunteers to former communist countries. They have completed over US$100 million worth of pro bono work, in countries as diverse as Russia, Hungary, and Moldova (see www.fsvc.org).

Cooperation is especially important at the regional level, helping individual countries to achieve a critical mass in scientific subjects. Fellowship programs to train energy analysts in developing countries have been established in prestigious universities in several countries in Asia, Africa, and Latin America, for example. The University Science, Humanities and Engineering Partnerships in Africa (USHEPiA) is also doing groundbreaking work in Africa (see Box 7).

International networks, meanwhile, provide promising opportunities for promoting

---

[9] This is well documented in the Third International Math and Science Study (TIMSS) by the US Department of Education. Please read *Pursuing Excellence: A Study of US Twelfth-Grade Mathematics and Science Achievement in International Context*. More information can be found at www.nces.ed.gov/timss/.

scientific innovation appropriate to the needs of developing countries. The Consultative Group on International Agricultural Research (CGIAR) is an example of a global program of research on agricultural issues having direct relevance to developing countries, such as rice production, food policy, agroforestry, and irrigation. The World Bank and three other United Nations agencies established the CGIAR in 1971. The network owes its existence and continuation to the financial support of multilateral donors, amounting to some US$300 million per year. Many of its achievements, ranging from the development of new rice varieties that sparked the Green Revolution to appropriate methods of soil and water conservation, represent international public goods that are unlikely to have evolved without concerted action.

International research centers such as those in the CGIAR network are sometimes criticized for failing to build scientific capacity within their host countries. The Task Force does not believe this is a valid observation. CGIAR centers, for example, have helped train more than 50,000 scientists in developing countries. But we believe more can be done to ensure that any investment in scientific capacity reinforces, rather than competes with, ongoing national efforts—an approach that will be further enhanced as national responses become more focused and coordinated. Local counterpart institutions, working in conjunction with internationally funded centers, can greatly enhance the value of international networks. Such cooperation gives local institutions an entree into the global research world and greatly spurs local efforts.

The Indian Institutes of Technology provide one example of beneficial crossovers from the international to a national science community. Five institutes were established in the early 1950s as "institutions of national importance," modeled explicitly after the best examples of technical higher education from

Germany, Russia, the United Kingdom, and the United States. Throughout the 1960s each of the institutes was heavily funded by a different country, and staffed by top-ranking faculty from both India and the funding country. Today the Indian Institutes of Technology enjoy not only national, but also international, prominence in several technical fields, operating successfully as Indian rather than as international institutions.

Reform of the International Intellectual Property Rights Regime

As more countries participate in the global economy, protection for the results of investment in knowledge creation has become increasingly important. Currently, however, most patents protect advances made in industrial countries, and licensing fees for product development based on new inventions are often prohibitively high. Universities and research institutes in developing countries therefore face significant financial barriers to research and, in the future, whole regions may find themselves cut off from participation in the global network of innovators.

Although this problem is not yet serious, there is growing recognition that it is likely to become so as the international intellectual property regime becomes more formalized. (The World Science Conference in Budapest, for example, was dominated by intellectual property issues.) Wider use of a sliding scale for licensing agreements, taking into account a country's level of development, would be helpful. Alternatively, these countries could purchase, perhaps with a subsidy from an international organization, a countrywide site license for access to software and particular research techniques. Another possibility would be to promote North–South joint ventures in which developed- and developing-country participants earn and share intellectual property rights. Advances in this area will need to be carefully thought through from the point of view of both the developing country and the intellectual property holder. Arrangements that do not give the property holder clear protection regarding the resale of technology are unlikely to be sustainable.

In this area, in particular, developing countries need to adopt emerging best practices from the industrialized world. The United Kingdom's National Endowment for Science, Technology and the Arts (NESTA),[10] for example, has explicitly committed itself to exploring creative partnerships with innovators where, in exchange for bearing some of the risk and providing financial support, NESTA obtains a percentage of the intellectual property rights. Profits are fed back into the funding loop. Where models do not exist, however, developing countries should be prepared to innovate. The knowledge economy will demand new and quite different institutions—and these may come more quickly in emergent than in mature economies.

Strategies for Scientific Development

The capacity to carry out scientific research is extremely limited in many developing countries. While not every country needs to conduct basic research in every field, each country must consider the types of scientific and technological research that can directly contribute to its development. In view of the costs and other difficulties, perhaps the right question to ask is: what is the *minimum* level of scientific and technological capacity necessary to achieve national goals?

At the very least, every country needs to be able to turn to a small corps of its own citizens for informed guidance and expert advice about scientific and technological developments. In addition to people who can choose wisely among technologies, there is a need to support and promote people who can begin to build scientific self-reliance. International collaboration is important in achieving this—with regional cooperation essential for those smaller countries in which a research university is not practical (see Box 2, Chapter 1). Selective excellence is also an important strategy, where countries focus on building strength in a few selected scientific disciplines—which should correspond closely with a country's needs and its comparative research advantage. For example, a country with a long coastline might naturally gravitate toward marine biology, while countries subject to volcanic eruptions and earthquakes would want experts in soil mechanics and construction engineers skilled in designing earthquake-resistant structures.

On a global level, market forces are a crucial determinant of the allocation of scientific effort among competing substantive issues. AIDS and malaria each claim roughly as many lives a year, but AIDS is far more prevalent in richer countries than malaria, and receives far more research funding. The lack of effective demand also explains the paucity of research in other areas that have great potential for improving the living standards of the world's poor. Examples include research into chimney and other ventilation systems that would protect household members (mainly women and young children) from respiratory ailments and eye problems caused by indoor pollution; and the development of nonsterile varieties of hybrid corn and of wheat, rice, and corn varieties that can better fix nitrogen in the soil and thereby reduce the use of chemical fertilizers.

Achieving a tighter focus on national, regional, and even global research priorities will inevitably involve multiple sets of stakehold-

---

[10] http://www.nesta.org

ers. While the World Health Organization has a global role, so too does the wider international donor community—who usually have access to substantial high-quality science and technology expertise and resources. The more coordinated response recently outlined by African science ministers (see Box 7) also offers a greatly extended opportunity to focus efforts, as do initiatives such as those of the William H. and Melinda Gates Foundation, which recently donated US$50 million for work on a malaria vaccine. National governments, too, can play a role. For example, the science and technology community in the United Kingdom has seen a shift, in barely a decade, from a research agenda entirely defined by scientists and researchers to one driven more by the outputs that the government, as the client, wants to buy.

Scientists and researchers themselves can also help drive the research agenda on global priorities. This century has seen many examples of moral leadership by scientists, most recently from Nobel prizewinner Joseph Rotblat of Pugwash (who recently argued that scientists should take the equivalent of a Hippocratic oath). Within higher education institutions—especially research universities—scientists have a great deal of academic freedom and insulation from commercial pressures. Scientists from all countries have a responsibility to use this privilege, which is heavily funded by society, for society's good. The work of scientists constantly challenges us, with its potential to benefit humanity, or to harm it. Nuclear technology can be simultaneously seen as a curse or a blessing, offering a formidable weapon but also a treatment for cancer and a source of plentiful electricity. The work of scientists in the field of genetics holds before us the opportunity to tackle age-old diseases, while it also augurs the specter of genetic selection. Each advance gives humanity choices that require a special responsibility from scientists.

Finally there is the public. There is a strong case for extensive and effective public communication about science, thereby enhancing cultural support for science and technology, and about its content—for example, safer sex campaigns based on scientific understanding of sexually transmitted diseases such as HIV. Public involvement in science must go further than this. If science is in part a public good that needs to be at least partly publicly funded, then the public has a clear interest in scientific objectives, processes, and outcomes. Strategies to support scientific development will need to encourage the creation of an open and accountable scientific community and recognize the importance of public support for continued scientific development.

University–Industry Cooperation

Developing countries have a great potential for strengthening science and technology links between higher education institutions and industry. Universities are predominantly nonproprietary settings and, because they bring together representatives of all disciplines into a single place, they provide fertile grounds for cross-pollination. Commercial, specialized research centers also produce top-notch research, but their capacity is sometimes limited by the narrowness of their focus. The development of new technologies consists of three types of interconnected activities: (i) research, (ii) technology development and adaptation, and (iii) production and marketing. The largest role for universities is in carrying out the initial research, but subsequent product development and distribution often result in a fruitful interplay between universities and industry. In many developed countries an increasing number of companies are spinning off from universities, a process that happens when researchers are encouraged to look for commercial applications of their work. Because some technical expertise can be acquired only through learning-by-doing, industrial apprenticeships are also an effective means of training new cadres of highly skilled workers. In fact, the very nature of the knowledge revolution, and the intimate links between, for example, academia and the Internet or biotechnology, have helped shape a different set of cultural values around such collaboration. Where industry's relationship with universities was once based on geographical links or the interests of alumni, today's collaborators are seeing a "death of distance" as technology enables collaborations to work at huge distances. This culture can, in due course, extend benefits to developing countries.

Many countries—Argentina, Brazil, Chile, China, Colombia, the Arab Republic of Egypt, India, Kenya, Malaysia, and Nigeria, among others—have taken active steps to forge stronger links between their academic and industrial sectors. In Brazil, this interaction resulted in the development of an alternative fuel that replaced half the country's use of gasoline automobiles with renewable, domestic sources of energy. As another example, high rates of maternal mortality in rural areas in India caused by lack of access to blood transfusions inspired the development, in one medical research center, of low-cost plastics that could resist the inherent corrosiveness of blood and be used for storing blood. The international marketing of this product has been handled in a completely commercial manner, with some of the proceeds being used to subsidize local use of the product.

Conclusions

The problem of insufficient scientific capacity in developing countries is acute, but it is not insurmountable. Higher education has played a leading role in bringing about im-

pressive scientific achievements under difficult circumstances in various parts of the developing world. Generally, these achievements have arisen as a result of an early, deep, and sustained commitment to particular areas of science or technology.

Notwithstanding the success stories, developing countries are falling further behind industrial countries in terms of their science and technology capacities and achievements. Perhaps the most disturbing aspect of this trend is that many areas of scientific inquiry that hold great promise for the development of international public goods are receiving inadequate attention. These problems bode ill for social and economic development, and suggest a further widening of global inequality in standards of living. Many very useful discoveries end up sidelined because of a lack of support either from business or government, not because they are inherently inapplicable. In the case of the Baylis wind-up radio that requires neither outside sources of electricity nor batteries—a very popular product manufactured in South Africa that has brought news and information to many poor families—the inventor spent long, frustrating years trying to raise the interest of manufacturers. This useful invention would still remain unknown were it not for some seed money from the British government.

Inadequate resources (both physical and human) for science education, and the absence of key values and traditions that promote effective scientific inquiry and training, are among the main causes of the deteriorating position of developing countries in the sciences. We have suggested some means by which higher education institutions and governments can address these problems. Strong international leadership that provides sustained intellectual and financial support for strengthening the scientific capacity of developing countries is also urgently needed. Equally important are efforts to strengthen scientific links between institutions of higher education in developing countries and centers of scientific excellence worldwide.

The key question that will exercise policymakers in developing countries is "where should promoting science and technology higher education rank in the long list of priorities for resources?" The answer will vary from country to country. Science and technology are moving with extraordinary speed. Countries such as India and many of the Southeast Asian economies now play a strong role in the development of software and hardware. With the many incalculable spin-off benefits yielded by technologies such as the Internet, the world is entering the future before our eyes. Playing a role in that future requires every developing country to think strategically about how their inevitably limited resources for science and technology higher education might best be deployed to the advantage of future generations.

Chapter 6 | The Importance of General Education

The illiterate of the 21st century will not be those who cannot read and write, but those who cannot learn, unlearn and relearn.

Alvin Toffler (1928-)

In the modern world, the importance of highly specialized scientific and technical education is well recognized. But a broad education is also important, and this chapter makes the case for liberal or general education (the terms are used interchangeably) at the university level in developing countries. This argument may seem unusual and perhaps also controversial, but it reflects the Task Force's view that this type of education could play a more constructive role than is commonly realized in helping developing countries to achieve their long-term socio-economic goals.

A higher education system should meet many different goals. These include:

- satisfying demand from students for an increasingly sophisticated and rewarding education;

- training the people needed to run a modern society and contribute to its further advancement;

- providing a forum in which a society can examine its problems and identify appropriate solutions; and

- offering a setting in which a society's culture and values can be studied and developed.

In a stratified higher education system, institutions of different types fill these needs in different ways. Professional and vocational schools meet some needs, while open universities and distance-learning institutions satisfy others. However, developing countries need to be sure that some of their institutions are providing a sufficient breadth of education to give students the abilities that are needed in a rapidly changing world. A general education is an excellent form of preparation for the flexible, knowledge-based careers that increasingly dominate the upper tiers of the modern labor force. With knowledge growing at unprecedented rates, higher education systems must equip students with the ability to manage and assimilate greatly expanded quantities of information. A specific expertise in technology will almost inevitably become obsolete. The ability to learn, however, will continue to provide valuable insurance against the vagaries of a rapidly changing economic environment.

What Is a General or Liberal Education?

A general or liberal education has been defined as "a curriculum [or part of a curriculum] aimed at imparting general knowledge and developing general intellectual capacities in contrast to a professional, vocational or technical curriculum." It is characterized by its focus on "the whole development of an individual, apart from his occupational training. It includes the civilizing of his life purposes, the refining of his emotional reactions, and the maturing of his understanding of the nature of things according to the best knowledge of our time."[11] These words were written over 50 years ago (today one would use more gender-neutral language).

There are a variety of opinions regarding the characteristics of a liberally educated person. A recent formulation by a member of our Task Force describes such a person as someone who:

- can think and write clearly, effectively, and critically, and who can communicate with precision, cogency, and force;

- has a critical appreciation of the ways in which we gain knowledge and understanding of the universe, of society, and of ourselves;

- has a broad knowledge of other cultures and other times, and is able to make decisions based on reference to the wider world and to the historical forces that have shaped it;

- has some understanding of and experience in thinking systematically about moral and ethical problems; and

- has achieved depth in some field of knowledge.

This definition focuses on cognitive skills. It concerns teaching people to think and to learn. It also stresses breadth of knowledge across a number of disciplines. A liberally educated person should have an informed acquaintance with the mathematical and experimental methods of the physical and biological sciences; with the main forms of analysis and the historical and quantitative techniques needed to investigate the development of a modern society; with some of the important scholarly, literary, and artistic achievements of the past; and with humanity's major religious and philosophical concepts. A liberal education should leave students excited by the world of learning and prepared to continue their education, both in the short term—through in-depth study of a specialist discipline—and in the long term as they continually refresh their knowledge in formal and informal ways, through the process of lifelong learning.

In some parts of the world, the term "liberal education" has a conservative or traditional connotation, implying a particular way of looking at the world. The Task Force, however, is not advocating the universal application of a particular curriculum or teaching method across different cultures. Instead, it is recommending that each country design its own general curriculum to fit the structure and values of its higher education system. Indeed, the exercise of developing a national—though not nationalistic—general education curriculum should be socially useful, requiring a country to examine the state and direction of human knowledge and establish priorities for its higher education system.

As they design and impart a sound, comprehensive educational foundation, educators need to:

- take into account their own economic, social, political, and institutional environment;

- look for the common unifying themes that pull together a curriculum and make it more than an arbitrary combination of alternative elements;

- move beyond limits of traditional disciplinary boundaries to explore the relationships among different subjects and ways of thinking about the world;

---

[11] José Ortega y Gasset, *Mission of the University*. London: Kegan Paul, Trench, Trubner, 1946, p.1. The quotes are the introductory words of Leo Nostrand, the translator.

Box 9

Home-Grown and Breaking New Ground: Another BRAC Initiative

The Bangladesh Rural Advancement Committee, or BRAC, is justly celebrated as one of the developing world's most impressive nongovernmental organizations (NGOs). Describing itself as a "national private development organization," BRAC has approximately 17,000 regular staff and more than 30,000 part-time teachers covering 50,000 villages. The vast majority of its clients are women, and for the past 27 years it has been making loans to the rural poor and other marginalized populations, as well as offering services including education, training, healthcare, and family planning. The BRAC health program alone covers some 25 million people, while 1.2 million poor children now receive primary education through its education program. About 85,000 groups of the landless poor, with a membership of over 3 million, have also been organized. BRAC's annual budget, 60 percent of which is self-generated, is now more than US$130 million. Among its latest initiatives is an attempt to set up an entirely new liberal arts university, based on an identification of local needs and aspirations.

BRAC started with a significant program of research among potential employers, students, and parents, as well as successful local universities. BRAC wanted to identify an approach for the proposed university that would ensure not only financial viability through good initial enrollment rates, but that would also ensure that the university's graduate stream would prove attractive to prospective local employers; this, in turn, would link back to maintaining enrollment on an ongoing basis. This initiative took place in the context of BRAC's wider developmental aims for Bangladesh. These include a particular focus on improving the situation and influence of women, from the household level to the labor market.

BRAC's research phase threw up several interesting insights. For example, employers initially told BRAC that they sought programs with a strong technical focus, for example in biology, technology, management, and computer science. They wanted graduates who were "ready to go." However, on further probing, it emerged that local employers' interests were in fact centered on obtaining a stream of graduates who could demonstrate a strong array of analytical skills and a solid grounding in writing, communication, and presentation skills, in addition to their technical expertise. Their concern—in common with many, if not most, modern employers who are considering graduates as employees—was to seek out workers with a good ability to analyze and think through complexity, a useful level of English language skills, and a well-rounded ability to think independently and take initiative. This is the very combination of general and specialist skills argued for throughout this report.

A study of the competition—successful local private universities—showed two very popular programs: computer science and business administration (a subject that has come to be perceived as a "gilt-edged degree" by students and employers alike). Because of the strong cultural influence they still exert, parents of prospective students were also interviewed about their concerns. Their biggest concern—as with all parents—was quality. They wished to be reassured that the quality of the university education offered was internationally competitive. Like the prospective employers, parents were also emphatic about the importance of English language skills. Some even stated that they would not send their children to a private university where courses were taught in Bengali. Further, parents wished to see their daughters take up higher education (and most of BRAC's membership base is female), but were concerned that current educational possibili-

continued...

Box 9 continued

ties meant their daughters might have to look abroad for good study options. This emphasizes one of the potential roles that educational reform can play in promoting gender equity.

Although BRAC wished to broaden student enrollment among its membership base, there was also recognition that for many of these poorer Bangladeshis, there were issues around both expense and low educational attainment levels. The proposed fees, of between US$1,500 to US$2,000 per annum, are in keeping with the upper limit on tuition levels observed at other private universities in Bangladesh, such as North–South University and Independent University. In other words, the tuition fees would be much more than those charged by the public university system (which are entirely nominal at around 50 cents per year; apparently the cost of collecting this fee exceeds the amount collected), but not more than other private universities supplying a more traditional education with early specialization.

A real issue remains with respect to how many can satisfy the test and entry requirements. BRAC University therefore intends to take the practical approach and enroll some, but not all, poor students (with partial-to-full scholarships reserved for a modest percentage of the student population in the four-year program). There is also a plan to create an endowment to help fund these scholarships—the rest will involve cross-subsidies from tuition receipts—while the bulk of students will come from lower-middle-, middle-, and upper-middle-class families.

Through an exhaustive process of research among the main stakeholders, BRAC's feasibility study for a university has developed into what is, in effect, an interesting new hybrid appropriate to developing world contexts. BRAC intends to place an emphasis on practical and job-related skills while also honing more generally portable analytical and English language skills. The proposed curriculum includes two years of liberal arts, which will also cover general skills, including writing, communication, presentation, and analysis. The core curriculum has courses in development economics, history, sociology, and the sciences (physics or biology) in addition to mathematics and English. Many of these courses would have a strong "development studies" orientation—another way in which the curriculum is customized to national needs.

These two years of liberal arts are then followed by two years of specialized technical training (as distinct from, for example, the more common pattern of four years' general education with a major and electives, as seen in the United States). In this combination there lies a fusion between old and new that more closely reflects students' and employers' aspirations for both a better general education and an ability to take up jobs requiring technical skills.

While surveys indicated a strong demand for a BRAC University on the part of students, the biggest obstacle to be overcome is finding good faculty, especially given that the plan requires adoption of a more modern and active approach to teaching than the traditional "lecture-from-notes" method, where students are asked to simply memorize and then regurgitate facts. It is regrettable that, while the application to become a private university was lodged with the Ministry of Education early in 1997, confirmation has yet to be achieved. This is in part due to an ongoing realignment of higher education priorities in the country.

BRAC website: http://www.brac.net

- concentrate on the delivery, not simply the content, of the curriculum, moving beyond rote learning to give students a deeper, more engaged and meaningful exposure to the rich and varied world of intellectual pursuits.

Who Should Receive a Liberal Education?

Depending on the student and his or her goals, different levels of general education are possible. These include:

- a basic grounding for all higher education students, whatever type of institution they attend or course they study;

- a discrete and substantial component of general education, which helps broaden the experience of students engaged in specialist, professional, or technical study; and

- an intensive general education curriculum that provides exceptionally promising, intellectually oriented students with a solid basis for their careers or for advanced specialist study.

Within a differentiated higher education system, the more intensive programs will almost certainly be offered at the most selective universities, with the majority of professional, scientific, and technical courses remaining more narrowly focused. Selective universities prepare many of those who aspire to leadership roles, and for them a preparation for only the initial stages of a career is no longer sufficient. Path-finding individuals must update and acquire new, and often very different, skills. General education is ideally suited to this process of lifelong learning, providing the cognitive orientation and skills needed to facilitate continual re-education.

However, general education should not be confined to a few traditional universities. The capacity for lifelong learning is increasingly important for the many people who face major career shifts. Mature students, for instance, often return to education with a determination to change the direction of their lives. Many look for study opportunities outside the traditional university system, for example, through distance learning. As noted earlier, women also commonly leave the labor force because of family obligations. Flexibility and the ability to learn new skills have a significant impact on how successfully they return, often after a decade or more.

Increasing, the supply of general education can also help to promote social equity and mobility. In some countries, such as parts of Africa, India, and Pakistan, a narrow and privileged segment of the population has already received its broad education at elite secondary institutions that offer elaborate and extensive general education programs. As higher education systems expand, they must become more tolerant at points of entry, while ensuring that quality at the point of exit is maintained. This means shouldering an increased share of the burden of providing general education, and ensuring that those who have not had a broad secondary education have the chance to catch up and fulfil their potential.

Why Is General Education Relevant for Developing Countries?

Does general education deserve support in the developing world, or is it just a luxury for the wealthy countries? The Task Force is convinced that general education has a clear, practical impact on society, well beyond the love of learning and human development it promotes.

Both industrial and developing countries need leaders, educated citizens, and trained workers for industry, government and politics, and academia. A liberal education enhances the chances that individuals will be able to fulfil these roles with distinction. At present, many developing countries are overly dependent on the industrial countries to offer a broadly based education to a few of their (richer) citizens. Women are especially disadvantaged by this state of affairs, with many families, especially those in conservative societies, frowning upon young women traveling abroad to study.

General education also has a clear practical impact on a society. It can promote responsible citizenship, ethical behavior, educational ambition, professional development in a broad range of fields, and even global integration. It prevents students from becoming "balkanized" in narrowly focused disciplines and fosters cohesion across cohorts whose more talented and motivated students are familiarized with a core body of knowledge, some of which is unique to their own culture and some of which is universal. General education also promotes civil society through its contribution to broad-mindedness, critical thinking, and communication skills, all of which are essential elements of effective participatory democracy. It should foster tolerance and ethical values, helping to encourage the social awareness and philanthropy that are vital to a society's health and stability.

General education is also important in the development process. It helps society look at the social and ethical questions raised by new development policies and projects, ensuring that a country's long-term interests are given priority over short-term gains. Within the education sector, it encourages countries to define national intellectual priorities and promote an intellectual identity through the process of defining the content of a general curriculum that meets nationally specific needs.

Finally, better general education may help reduce the brain drain. Providing in-country general education is less expensive than sending undergraduates abroad. For example, there are roughly 350,000 developing-country graduate and undergraduate students in the United States alone, at a total cost of approximately US$10 billion per year, which exceeds the individual gross national product of more than half the world's countries. Students who are educated at home are more likely to remain at home, perhaps even for graduate study. Even in cases where students go abroad for graduate study—and that is the largest group—they are more likely to want to return to a society that has offered them an intellectually stimulating environment during their undergraduate career.

What Are the Obstacles?

In the developing world, the concept of liberal education is associated with a variety of obstacles. While some are economic, the philosophical ones may be more significant.

The first obstacle is the issue of costs and benefits. High-quality liberal education is not inexpensive. It requires more varied faculty resources, interactive rather than passive teaching techniques, seminars in place of lectures, and perhaps a longer period spent in school. But the payoff to a high-quality liberal education is not immediate, and it has a large nonpecuniary component that is difficult to measure.

Funding is clearly problematic, but the more extensive general education programs are not meant for all, or even the majority, of students. They should be aimed at the brightest and most highly motivated in any cohort, with a broader cross-section of students offered less intensive forms of general education. The Task Force attaches great importance to this, as it is far less expensive and time-consuming than offering such an education to all.

Aiming higher education programs at the brightest and most motivated students should not be objectionable or characterized as elitism in the old sense. First, advantage should accrue to an individual because of intellectual capacities and efforts, and not because of social class or wealth. Second, the Task Force advocates special programs for disadvantaged groups at all stages of education, so that these citizens are increasingly able to take advantage of the best educational opportunities. Third, we recognize the value of some general education in nearly all forms of higher education, with specific programs designed and modified for different types of student and school.

These considerations will not eliminate financial concerns, but they should lessen the problem. However, the problem of different abilities remains. Not all individuals are qualified for the same training or the same tasks, given that some tasks are more difficult than others. This implies that inequalities in some areas are a natural outcome. Educating the most able for positions of leadership in all spheres of life has to be in the national interest; it is a major aspect of stratification.

We have already noted that, while the connection between the short-term needs of the labor market and general education may be weak, in the longer run general education is an excellent investment for both individuals and nations. Some believe that general education is at odds with the trend toward increasing specialization within the labor force, especially the upper tiers. On the contrary, high-quality general education strengthens disciplinary specialization by providing a solid foundation for advanced learning and specialization. It also provides a common intellectual currency for interaction among individuals with diverse specializations.

Because general education involves in-depth and open examination of ideas and assumptions of all kinds, it sometimes appears threatening to those who have an interest in preserving the status quo. That desire, however, represents the very opposite of development. Highlighting the value of liberal education for effective leadership may also pose an implicit challenge to the credentials of leaders who themselves received different training, and sometimes very little formal education. Of course, a more educated leadership is one indicator of socioeconomic progress.

Some will ask why market forces have not created a greater supply of general education if it offers so many benefits. The reasons relate to a disparity between the long-term public interest and short-term needs (see Chapter 2). General education is not part of the academic tradition in most developing countries. In addition, students are interested in immediate, and perhaps more certain, returns, especially when education loans and scholarships are difficult to obtain. High-quality general education tends to be expensive, deterring its provision in both public and private institutions. However, especially in the long run, societies will do well to serve the public interest even if market forces do not create the necessary incentives. General education is, in this sense, in the same category as basic research or equitable access.

Conclusions

In some countries, the term "liberal education" recalls colonial domination and education. This is unfortunate. While this particular method of education has Western roots, our emphasis is on an educational approach developed by each country, paying specific attention to its own culture and its particular needs. The goal for all countries is similar—a broad, flexible, interactive education that addresses the whole human being—but the road to achieving this goal is unique and cannot simply be transplanted from one country to another. The time has come for national debates to begin. What is an educated person? Once a country has accepted the general education concept, what are the implications for curricula and other aspects of training?

This debate is under way in a number of developing countries. Some institutions in India, the Republic of Korea, Nigeria, Pakistan, the Philippines, parts of Latin America, and some others already practice general education, although the quality of these efforts is uneven. Most recently, the National University of Singapore has engaged a major curricular review with the intention of creating a new core curriculum (see Box 10). Leaders from both government and education concluded that national preparation for the knowledge-based world required soundly designed liberal education, as opposed to exclusive emphasis on specialist, and usually technical, subjects. The Task Force hopes this interest in general education will continue to spread across the developing world, and that many more countries will develop increasingly broad, flexible, and innovative curricula.

Box 10

Singapore's Curriculum Renewal for National Goals

In the summer of 1999 the National University of Singapore (NUS) launched its new curriculum for selected undergraduates. This was the result of lengthy consultations that began in 1997, and brought in the views of leading scholars drawn from several elite universities around the world.

Singapore sought to ensure that its future graduates could walk proudly alongside any graduate from the more established schools. They strove to develop the personal, intellectual, and leadership qualities of students to equip them to excel in life.

Key to the new curriculum is exposing students to various schools of thought, helping them to understand, for example, how a physicist, a biologist, and a historian approach problems. Students select their core area of study, but are also obliged to select courses from an area outside their field.

The curriculum attempts to:

• synthesize and integrate knowledge from diverse disciplines, to establish a connection between all human knowledge, and

• infuse students with a concrete understanding of the process of human creativity.

It includes these subjects:

• One module each from the Writing Program and History

• Select modules from the Humanities and Social Sciences and from areas of Science and Mathematics.

The new curriculum has already drawn praise from the private sector. "The Core Curriculum program at NUS is designed to deliver well rounded graduates, who are lateral thinkers, innovative, articulate and groomed to lead," said S. Nasim, Managing Director, Meinhardt (Singapore) Pte Ltd., "comparable to the best graduates of Harvard or MIT. They will be snapped up like hotcakes by industry."

The Core Curriculum, National University of Singapore, 1999–2000

Conclusions

Education is not the filling of a pail, but the lighting of a fire.

W. B. Yeats (1865–1939)

Although developing countries contain more than 80 percent of the world's population, they account for just half of its higher education students, and for a far smaller proportion of those with access to high-quality higher education. Overcoming these gaps is a daunting challenge that will require a concerted effort between developing and developed countries.

In this concluding chapter we return to the three core questions asked in the Introduction, summarizing the report by synthesizing the answers to each question as they cut across the various chapters.

- What is the role of higher education in supporting and enhancing the process of economic and social development?

- What are the major obstacles that higher education faces in developing countries?

- How can these obstacles best be overcome?

The preceding chapters broke these overarching questions into a set of manageable and reasonably self-contained—though not exhaustive—issues. We have tried to frame each issue and to explain its importance today and, more significantly, the role it is likely to play in the twenty-first century. We have concentrated on what higher education offers society as a whole, emphasizing those aspects of higher education where the public has interests that are distinctly different from or more extensive than private interests.

It is clear that higher education institutions come in all shapes and sizes, and this means that solutions will need to be organic. A standard set of remedies is also doomed to fail when countries are so diverse. Despite this diversity, the main objective of the Task Force has been to determine strategies for higher education reform, as well as general guidelines and principles for assessing the operation of higher education systems and institutions. These benchmarks offer guidance for informed dialogue aimed at educational reform—helping to cut through the often confusing thicket of institutions and practices. Our analysis and conclusions are a blend of research and discussion with colleagues from around the world and the professional expertise of our members. We have consciously tried not to emphasize the lessons of one country at the expense of others.

This report's findings can be boiled down to two simple conclusions.

- *Significant obstacles.* Higher education must overcome formidable impediments if it is to realize its potential contribution to society. Some of these impediments—such as demographic change, fiscal stringency, and the knowledge revolution—are determined by external forces of considerable power and must be taken as given. Others can be removed or mitigated. One example is the ineffective management that plagues so much of higher education, yet this is largely within the overlapping domains of higher education institutions and national governments to overcome. Change will not be easy. The problems are deep-seated, and efforts to rationalize and strengthen systems and institutions will require sustained effort. This work will certainly span several political cycles in most countries.

- *Hope for progress.* The problems facing higher education are not insurmountable. Existing resources can be used more effectively, and there are already a number of areas in which the mobilization of additional resources, both economic and political, will result in big gains. Conversely, countries that continue to neglect higher education will tend to become increasingly marginalized in the world economy, suffer from relatively slow social and political progress, and find it ever more difficult to catch up. Progress is most likely in countries that develop a clear vision of what higher education can contribute to the public interest. Piecemeal fixes must be avoided in favor of a holistic approach, focusing on the complementary and mutually reinforcing nature of a range of possible solutions.

How Higher Education Supports Development

Statistical analysis, case study, and common observation all point to the fundamental importance of higher education to development. Higher education promotes the following:

- *Income growth.* The vitality of higher education is a fundamental—and increasingly important—determinant of a nation's position in the world economy. It contributes to labor productivity, entrepreneurial energy, and quality of life; enhances social mobility; encourages political participation;

strengthens civil society; and promotes democratic governance. It does this by creating public goods such as new knowledge—a catalyst for rapid development—and by providing a safe space for the free and open discussion of the values that define the character of a nation's development. Economic growth is a powerful determinant of poverty alleviation and improvements in people's lives. Higher education's contribution to growth, therefore, means better living standards for people at all levels of a society.

- *Enlightened leaders.* Higher education can give leaders the confidence, flexibility, breadth of knowledge, and technical skills needed to effectively confront the economic and political realities of the twenty-first century. It also generates cadres of well-trained teachers for all levels of the education system.

- *Expanding choices.* Development is fundamentally concerned with expanding the choices people can make. As such, an accessible higher education system—offering a wide range of quality options for study—is a major achievement, bolstering social mobility and helping the talented to fulfil their potential.

- *Increasingly relevant skills.* Higher education is absolutely necessary for training scientists, engineers, and others to help invent, adopt, and operate modern technology in all sectors. When scientists in developing countries are inspired to define and address local problems, they are likely to contribute to appropriate solutions in such vital areas as environmental protection, the prevention and treatment of illness, industrial expansion, and infrastructure provision.

These benefits are not automatic. They are linked to the character of higher education systems and institutions, as well as to the broader social, political, and economic systems within which they are situated. Even a well-functioning higher education system, operating under the most favorable of circumstances, is not *sufficient* for social and economic development. But better higher education will certainly be *necessary* in most countries, if more vibrant development is to take place. Indeed in some countries, especially those with extremely low levels of per capita income, higher-education initiatives will not dominate the policy agenda for the foreseeable future. Higher education will remain important for these countries, but they may do best by relying, for the time being, on institutions outside their countries, possibly with donor assistance, as a prelude to building stronger higher education systems of their own.

We have not asked whether higher education matters more than other key sectors such as agriculture, health, transportation, and basic education. But we are absolutely confident that it is much more important to development than one would surmise from the comparative neglect it has received in most quarters of the international development community in recent decades. Higher education's benefits must now be recognized more widely so it can take its place in the mainstream of the international development agenda. The information revolution that is driving the new economy is dependent on educated and literate workers; and more than ever, the new ideas fueling this expansion have come from people with tertiary degrees.

The Major Obstacles

The experience of higher education in developing countries has been disappointing to date. Its contribution to social and economic development has not mirrored its accomplishments in developed countries. The signs of this failure are most apparent when judged by international standards as demanded by the emerging world economy. Poor educational quality, a dearth of significant contributions to knowledge, and a failure to advance the public interest are all too common.

Strategies for addressing these problems need to proceed from an understanding of their underlying roots. We believe higher education in many developing countries is significantly weighed down by four sets of conditions.

- *The absence of vision.* The social and economic importance of higher education systems, and of individual institutions within those systems, is insufficiently appreciated. Unlike primary and secondary education, there is little in the way of a shared vision about the nature and magnitude of the potential contribution of higher education to development. But this understanding is crucial to a sector that requires long-term investment in return for social benefits that are difficult to measure. Without it, higher education institutions are treated, essentially by default, in the same way as other large bureaucracies, leaving them without the power to make choices that improve their individual and collective performance.

- *Lack of political and financial commitment.* Policymakers face a host of pressing problems under conditions of severe resource constraints and highly competitive political settings. It's no surprise in such a policy environment that higher education often misses out. There is a common view that it is not deserving of political support because it is the preserve of the elite, who are eminently capable of taking care of themselves. While investment in higher education will surely benefit many already wealthy students, its social benefits outweigh this, raising a nation's average income and reducing its poverty. Meanwhile, demand is increasing at a great rate, creating complex challenges associated with managing the expansion of any system. Without significant national support and guidance for managing and planning expansion, quality inevitably suffers.

- *Conditions of initial disadvantage.* Higher education in developing countries is severely disadvantaged by its poor baseline. Knowledge begets knowledge. Fruitful scientific inquiry is often aided by having a suitable intellectual culture. And a critical mass of scholars and teachers is often required before higher education can thrive. Escaping this low-level trap necessarily requires substantial and wide-ranging improvements, rather than the all-too-frequent patchy and incremental steps.

- *The disruptions of globalization.* The best and brightest faculty and students will continue to be attracted to the wealthier countries, and competition for quality graduates will remain fierce. The money markets will ensure that economic fluctuations travel rapidly around the world, potentially jeopardizing institutional budgets when currencies collapse. Institutions are at great risk of falling behind if they do not keep up with the rest of the world in the information revolution and take advantage of the opportunities it offers. It is a two-sided coin, however, and information technology in the form of the Internet can ensure that universities are not pushed further outside the information network.

These ills will not cure themselves. They must be confronted now, and aggressively. Otherwise, developing countries will miss out on the powerful boost higher education can give to development, and will face increasingly daunting barriers to system improvement.

What To Do?

This report offers numerous suggestions for unleashing the potential of higher education's contribution to society. In doing so, our aim has been to stimulate and provoke, and to demonstrate that a menu of creative options exists. Higher education is, by its nature, optimistic and forward-looking. It is in this spirit that we offer our conclusions. In addition, a strategy for educational reform must be closely tailored to conditions in different countries—it makes little sense to endorse specific suggestions for application in any generic context. Policymakers must also be careful to do more than emulate developed-country models. Many richer countries have outdated systems that are also in need of reform. Developing countries have the opportunity to leapfrog outmoded models, planning for tomorrow's world, not yesterday's.

The Task Force's recommendations fall into two main categories: increasing resources, and improving the efficiency with which resources are used. A larger and more diversified resource base is needed for:

- improving educational infrastructure, especially computer and Internet access, scientific laboratories, and equipment, but also more traditional infrastructure such as libraries, classrooms, dormitories, and recreation and cultural facilities;

- the design, testing, and implementation of new curricula and academic programs, including the expansion or introduction of general education;

- the recruitment, retention, motivation, and long-term development of well-trained faculty;

- increasing access for economically and socially disadvantaged populations; and

- conducting more and better science education and research, both basic and applied.

Investment in the quality of secondary education is also needed to strengthen higher education, by improving the preparation of its new entrants. Also, if higher education institutions are more respected and accessible, secondary students will feel it is worthwhile to strive to attend them.

Although the Task Force urges international donors to increase their support for higher education, the majority of additional resources will necessarily have to come from within developing countries. There is no generally accepted formula for assigning responsibility for the generation of these resources, and the Task Force did not dwell on this important issue. Nevertheless, common sense suggests that beneficiaries should share responsibility, with students, private firms, and the public all included. Countries should focus on rational and effective use of existing resources, while remembering that outside partners are happier placing good money on top of good money. Institutions that squander resources and supply substandard education should not be surprised if they continue to find resource mobilization difficult.

The Task Force has highlighted a number of approaches to increasing the effectiveness with which resources are used. We believe that poor management is often the single greatest obstacle to stronger higher education. Management practices can be vastly improved by adhering to the principles of good institutional governance described in earlier chapters. Equally large gains can be enjoyed by designing a more rational and coordinated architecture for the system as a whole. This will help eliminate unnecessary duplication of effort, and cater to neglected social interests in areas such as curriculum, teaching materials, admissions processes, and informa-

tion systems. In meeting increased demand at a reasonable cost, new information technology affords remarkable opportunities. But more work needs to be done, especially in communicating how these opportunities can be advantageous. The public sector must also assume an increased role in providing constructive oversight for private institutions, thus helping to expose the system to greater internal competition, which is in itself an important driver for educational quality and managerial efficiency.

Perhaps the most natural starting point for higher education reform involves crafting a vision of a rational system—one based on verifiable facts and justifiable assumptions. To achieve this reform, a transparent and informed dialogue needs to take place, bringing together educators, industry, government, prospective students, and other relevant stakeholders. The system must be customized to fit a country's stage of development, political system, social structure, economic capacities, history, and culture. It is also important to avoid the process becoming too political, where a long wish list is produced and agreement is only for the least objectionable measures. A common vision should yield a framework to guide expansion and reform of higher education, while also organizing and managing the system in a way that is compatible with societal goals. This work will require long-term political and financial commitment, as well as high-level support to convince the public of the widespread importance of higher education.

Effective efforts to improve higher education in developing countries will reflect an overlapping division of labor among tertiary institutions, public policymakers, and international donors. As we have argued, institutions must take the lead in:

- strengthening their internal governance;

- improving the quality of existing academic programs such as those involving science and technology, and developing new programs, especially for the provision of general education and for helping bright and motivated students from disadvantaged backgrounds to overcome their academic deficits; and

- developing and motivating strong faculties.

Public policymakers have primary responsibility for:

- developing the architecture of a rational system of higher education and orchestrating its smooth operation in a manner that promotes both mass education and excellence;

- advancing the public interest in higher education, by:
  - providing special support for the natural sciences and the preservation of culture;
  - combating the tendency for financial concerns to sideline the principle of equal opportunity;
  - setting standards for degrees, and ensuring that the international trade in bogus credentials is brought to public attention;
  - generating and disseminating unbiased and relevant information about different institutions and degree programs;
  - protecting higher education as a venue for free and open discourse on a range of matters, even if the subjects are sensitive from society's point of view;
  - investing in the establishment of learning commons through which students from many institutions gain access to educational resources that individual schools sometimes cannot afford; typical

examples would be the Internet, libraries, and laboratory facilities;
  - regulating the private portion of higher education so as to encourage high standards while deterring abuses; and
  - addressing all planning issues in a global context, and considering how their systems can be linked to the wider world.

Finally, international *donors* would do well to support activities where the principal goals involve:

- catalyzing self-reliant and sustainable initiatives, including assessments of higher education systems and institutions;

- providing international public goods, which frequently arises from agricultural, medical, and environmental research, and can help foster cross-national research partnerships as well as student and faculty exchange programs; and

- promoting equity between and within countries through, for example, scholarship programs such as the Japanese-funded World Bank Scholars program, or by facilitating access to textbooks, computers, or other equipment.

The Task Force also emphasizes the importance of implementation. The field of international development is littered with good ideas that have yielded no fruit. Only rarely does the policy design process adequately anticipate the harsh and unforgiving realities found in the field. Projects routinely fail because they do not take adequate account of the competence and experience of the staff who will be relied upon to administer the policy or manage the project. Other projects fail because they do not involve stakeholders early in the planning process. We must—above all—be practical if we are to achieve successful reform.

The Bottom Line

Currently, two billion people live in the world's low-income countries. Their average income has a purchasing power of less than one-sixteenth of that enjoyed by the one billion people who live in the high-income countries. Even more astonishing is the ratio of the average income of the poorest and the richest one billion people on the planet: it is—conservatively—in the region of 1 to 80. The disturbing truth is that these enormous disparities are poised to grow even more extreme, impelled in large part by the progress of the knowledge revolution and the continuing brain drain.

The Task Force believes that strengthening higher education is a rational and feasible way for many countries to mitigate or avert further deterioration in their relative incomes, while positioning themselves on a higher and more sharply rising development trajectory.

Higher education cannot be developed to the exclusion of other policy initiatives. The development of infrastructure, better governance, public health improvements, trade reform, and financial market development—these and others will be needed as well. The benefits of higher education require a long gestation period. There may be shortcuts to establishing educational infrastructure, but influencing people to understand and convey higher education values and best practice will take decades, as opposed to a few years. For this reason the Task Force urges policymakers and donors—public and private, national and international—to waste no time. They must work with educational leaders and other key stakeholders to reposition higher education in developing countries. Only then will it produce larger and better trained pools of graduates and research of higher quality. The chance is simply too great to miss. As H.G. Wells said in *The Outline of History,* "Human history becomes more and more a race between education and catastrophe."

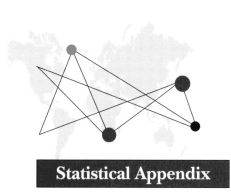

Statistical Appendix

I: International Data

International Statistics on Higher Education

As part of its work, the Secretariat for the Task Force on Higher Education undertook some independent research describing and analyzing cross-country patterns and trends in higher education. The Secretariat quickly discovered that UNESCO is the main, but not the only, source of basic data on higher education. The Secretariat also discovered that the data available tend to be sketchy in terms of the countries, years, and variables covered. In addition, the quality of the data is generally not well established.

Considerable effort went into assembling and testing the consistency of the cross-country data on higher education that were used in crafting portions of this report. These data are reproduced in this Appendix, in the interests of transparency, of providing readers with the raw data needed to facilitate further comparisons, and of sparing other researchers the time-consuming and tedious task of duplicating our efforts. To increase the value of this data supplement, the tables also include many standard higher education indicators not specifically relied upon in the report, as well as a number of general indicators of social and economic development.

In addition to the printed tables, the data are available electronically at www.thfe.net. It is anticipated that the data maintained on this website will be supplemented from time to time with additional cross-country information related to faculty compensation, international test scores, the nature of higher education laws and regulations, faculty-to-student ratios, indexes of public and private tuition, and numbers of public and private higher education institutions and average enrollment levels at each. In the course of preparing this report, we have particularly felt the absence of reliable data on the number of institutions of each type.

While assembling these data—all of which are derived from cross-country compilations that aimed at consistency—we have noted instances in which the figures given for a particular country do not match those independently available from sources within that country. For the sake of consistency, we have not made adjustments to the tables in such cases.

The tables cover 178 countries, which are listed alphabetically. They include data on enrollment, attainment, expenditure, research output, and several other items. Past and current values are reported for most indicators. Definitions for selected variables covered in the tables appear in the notes following the tables, as do references to the underlying data sources. Data aggregations for geographical regions and economic groupings have been calculated by weighting each country's data by population. When appropriate, weighting has been based on population subgroups.

Comparative and Historical Data on Education

The primary international source of data about education at all levels is UNESCO, the United Nations Educational, Scientific and Cultural Organization. UNESCO's Institute for Statistics collects and disseminates data on education from all countries and territories. A large amount of data are available from 1960 onward.

The Institute's main sources of information are official replies to questionnaires sent to countries annually. Three types of questionnaire are used: a questionnaire on education at pre-primary, first, and second levels; one on education at the tertiary level; and one on educational finance and expenditure. Information is collected on enrollment by level, gender, age, and field of study (for higher education); teaching staff by level and gender; illiteracy; educational attainment; and foreign students and graduates. The Institute for Statistics also reviews ad hoc national surveys designed to meet special needs, as well as other national publications and reports. They supplement these data with information from other international sources, including the Statistics and Population Division of the United Nations (for population, literacy, and attainment data), the World Bank (for GNP and other economic data), and the International Monetary Fund (for exchange rates).

Within individual countries, the responsibility for collecting data most commonly rests with the ministry of education or the central bureau of statistics. Questionnaires completed by schools are the basis for much of the information. Statistics on education spending are an exception, and may most often be obtained from central budgetary departments. Data on the adult population, such as level of educational attainment and literacy rates, are typically collected through national population censuses or through sample surveys.

The Institute for Statistics examines the data it receives, cross-referencing it with other sources and with the information maintained on its own database. If the new information appears problematic, they send a letter to the national authority cited as the source of the information and request a clarification. Their aim is to receive either corrected data, or an understanding of why the original data are correct despite the apparent discrepancy. If the issue is not resolved to their satisfaction, they may choose not to publish the data or to add a footnote expressing their concerns.

UNESCO organizes all these data and publishes it in its annual *Statistical Yearbook,* which is a major source of internationally comparable data on education. Many additional UNESCO publications draw on this data set or supplement it, and are listed within the yearbook. UNESCO data and publications lists are now easily accessed electronically on the UNESCO Institute for Statistics website, www.unesco.org. Computerized data are generally available for 1970 onward. In addition, the very detailed tables of the *Statistical Yearbook* exist as electronic spreadsheets that may be accessed through queries to the Institute for Statistics.

Additional sources of international educational data include the World Bank, which produces the *World Development Report,* and other United Nations offices, such as the United Nations Development Programme, which publishes the annual *Human Development Report.* A review of these publications demonstrates that almost all of their international data on education are ultimately attributed to UNESCO.

The most significant additional source of information on education is the Organisation for Economic Co-operation and Development (OECD). The OECD collects extensive data about its 29 member countries, all highly developed nations. Beginning in 1998, 13 developing nations also began contributing data to the OECD. OECD data on education are significantly more detailed than those that are usually available. For example, data on literacy are collected through a specialized instrument, the International Adult Literacy Survey, and reflect specific literacy skills of the adult population. At the tertiary level, OECD releases information otherwise not easily found, including information on private as well as public sources of funding; net enrollment ratios (as opposed to the gross enrollment ratios more commonly available); and teacher/student ratios at the tertiary level.

Some educational data are constructed by economists, based on census data distributed by UNESCO or a similar source. Robert Barro and Jong-Wha Lee, for example, have created estimates of educational attainment at 5-year intervals for more than 125 countries. Their estimation procedure begins with census information on school attainment, provided by individual governments and compiled by UNESCO and other sources. The census data provide benchmark numbers for a subset of dates under consideration. Missing cells are then filled in by using school enrollment ratios at various levels of schooling to estimate changes from the benchmarks to a more current date. The basic idea is that the flow of the enrolled population can be added to prior attainment levels to determine future levels. In this manner, full estimates of educational attainment can be obtained for most countries from the benchmark figures of one or more years, and from the reasonably complete data on school enrollment ratios.

In Barro and Lee's 1996 data set, for example, 310 census observations filled 35 percent of the 882 possible cells from 1960 to 1990 for 126 countries. The estimation procedure described above allowed them to construct a complete data set at 5-year intervals for 105 of these countries. The data are incomplete for the remaining 21 countries.

Limitations of the Data

Three main issues arise in using available national-level data on education: the comparability of the data, both across nations and over time; the consistency of the data; and the accuracy of the data.

Comparability

The problem of ensuring consistency of educational data across nations is a difficult one and is broadly recognized. In the *1998 Statistical Yearbook*, UNESCO authors repeatedly warn users of the need to take care when exercising comparisons between countries, and especially across groups of countries. Many of the differences between nations are detailed in charts that demonstrate differing years of educational entry, different years of schooling offered at the various levels, and different requirements about compulsory education. Readers are warned of particular issues, such as the counting of full-time and part-time teachers, which may vary across nations and have a strong and potentially misleading impact on data about student/teacher ratios.

Consistency

Efforts to deal with consistency problems have been under way for many years. Work on the standardization of educational statistics was first begun by UNESCO in 1926. Today's data reflect the impact of two sets of standards, the ISCED (International Standard Classification of Education), and the Recommendation Concerning the International Standardization of Educational Statistics that was adopted by UNESCO in 1958 and revised in 1978 to make it compatible with ISCED. ISCED provides general definitions of eight educational levels, and provides definitions for 518 programs of education and for 21 general fields of study. The recommendation details definitions and tabulations under four sections: statistics on illiteracy; on the educational attainment of the population; on enrollment, teachers, and educational institutions; and on educational finance. Together these standards provide some basis for creating greater international consistency for educational data.

That said, there is still reason to interpret much of the international educational data with caution. Definitions, coverage, and data-collection methods still differ across countries and may vary over time within countries, making interpretation difficult. The map of the world changes over time, and countries subject to major transitions, such as those of Eastern Europe, present problems of consistency and comparability. Periods of war and internal crises will obviously affect a country's ability to produce sound statistical information. Developing countries, particularly, vary in the amount of expertise and resources they choose to devote to statistical research on education.

Attempts to present information about educational financing across countries are particularly troubled by issues of comparability. One problem is the lack of complete information. Although many countries provide data on public expenditure on education, some limit their reporting to funds from the central ministry of education and neglect to report financial support from other branches and levels of government. Few nations report anything at all about private expenditure, despite the fact that, in many countries, private spending is a considerable factor at one or more levels of educational institutions.

Another problem that makes it difficult to compare financial information across nations is the blur between operating funds and capital expenditures. For example, one UNESCO table displaying data on operating expenditures for 108 countries had 12 footnotes indicating that, for those nations, capital expenses were also included in the figures.

A final—but particularly troublesome—issue in assessing financial data relates to the difficulties inherent in comparing different currencies across nations and over time. Without knowledge of inflationary trends within a country, for example, it can be difficult to compare the meaning of changing amounts of spending over time. Comparing spending across countries is even more difficult. Besides addressing inflationary pressures and currency conversion issues, it is necessary to adjust figures to compensate for differences in purchasing power from nation to nation over each year in question. Our research uncovered studies in which financial expenditures across the world were compared without properly considering each of these conversion issues.

Accuracy

The overall accuracy of educational data is another issue of serious concern. Jeffrey Puryear (1992) reports conversations in 1992 with experts at UNESCO who estimate that data from perhaps 70 countries—slightly fewer than half of UNESCO's member states—suffer from serious accuracy problems. Jean Drèze and Amartya Sen, in their monograph *India: Economic Development and Social Opportunity,* refuse to use official data on education, stating that these figures are known to be grossly inflated, partly due to the incentive that government employees at different levels have to report exaggerated figures. Although official statistics portray a gross enrollment ratio of 98–99 percent at the primary level, they present data from the census and a National Sample Survey that show that only 40–42 percent of rural girls between ages five and 14 attend school. India is obviously not alone in having officials overstate rates of enrollment for political reasons.

Data can also be unreliable due to poor assessment techniques. The data on illiteracy present one example. Few people realize that illiteracy rates are typically self-reported on population census forms, and that there is no universally accepted objective standard to evaluate literacy. Among the industrial countries, the OECD has collected data on functional literacy, but similar efforts have been lacking within the developing world. In some cases UNESCO considers attainment of a fourth-grade education to be sufficient evidence of literacy, even though no data are collected about the actual outputs of the educational process, or the skills typically demonstrated by students upon completing a given grade level. Measures such as literacy rates, which purport to reflect actual achievement, therefore need to be viewed somewhat skeptically.

In summary, though some efforts have been made to assess and correct issues of comparability and accuracy of national-level education data, much more work needs to be done. Given how extensively these data are relied upon, higher priority should be given to efforts in this area.

Statistical Appendix

TABLE A. GROSS ENROLLMENT RATIOS (%)

Country	Primary 1965	Primary 1995	Secondary 1965	Secondary 1995	Tertiary 1965	Tertiary 1975	Tertiary 1985	Tertiary 1995	Tertiary 1965 Male	Tertiary 1965 Female	Tertiary 1995 Male	Tertiary 1995 Female
Afghanistan	16	49	2	22	0	1	2	2	0	0	2	1
Albania		101		35				11			9	12
Algeria	68	107	7	62	1	3	9	12	1	0	14	10
Angola	41	77	5	12	0		1	1			1	0
Argentina	100	112	28	73	15	27	36	39	17	11	35	44
Armenia		82		79				14			13	14
Australia	99	103	62	147	16	24	28	72	22	10	70	74
Austria	100	100	52	103	9	19	27	47	13	4	46	47
Azerbaijan		104		77				18			18	18
Bahamas, The		95		89				24			15	33
Bahrain	69	108	45	97		2	10	20			16	24
Bangladesh	49	78	13	19	1	2	5	6	1	0	10	2
Barbados	100	99	52	97	3	10	19	29	3	3	24	35
Belarus		97		94				43			39	46
Belgium	100	102	75	146	15	23	31	56	19	10	56	56
Belize		122		49				1			1	1
Benin	34	72	3	16	0	1	3	3	0	0	4	1
Bermuda												
Bolivia	73	104	18	39	5	11	17	24	7	3	33	15
Botswana	65	112	3	64	0	1	2	5	0	0	6	5
Brazil	100	117	16	47	2	11	11	12	3	1	11	12
Brunei		108		77				7			5	8
Bulgaria		97		78				39			29	50
Burkina Faso	12	40	1	9		0	1	1			2	1
Burundi	26	51	1	7	0	0	1	1			1	1
Cambodia		126		26				2			3	1
Cameroon	94	87	5	26	0	1	2	4	1	0	7	1
Canada	100	103	56	107	26	39	56	90	33	20	83	98
Central African Republic	56	59	2	10	0	0	1	1	0	0	2	0
Chad	34	58	1	10	0	0	0	1			1	0
Chile	100	99	34	70	6	16	16	28	7	5	30	26
China	89	118	24	67			2	5			7	4
Colombia	84	114	17	67	3	8	13	17	5	1	17	18
Comoros	24	74	3	22			0	1			1	0
Congo, Dem. Rep. of	70	72	5	28	0	1	2	2	0	0	4	1
Congo, Rep. of	100	114	10	53	1	3	7	8	1	0	13	3
Costa Rica	100	107	24	50	6	18	23	33	7	5	36	30
Côte d'Ivoire		69		23			2	5			7	2
Croatia		86		82				28			28	28
Cuba		105		80				13			10	16
Cyprus	91		42		1	2	7	17	1	1	13	20
Czech Republic		104		99				22			23	21
Denmark	98	100	83	120	14	29	29	45	17	10	39	51
Djibouti		39		13				0			0	0
Dominican Republic	87	111	12	45	2	10	19	22	3	1	19	25
Ecuador	91	123	17	53	3	27	30	23	5	2	30	17
Egypt, Arab Rep. of	75	101	26	74	7	14	20	20	11	3	24	16
El Salvador	82	88	17	32	2	8	18	18	3	1	18	18
Eritrea		57		19				1			2	0
Estonia		91		104				38			35	41
Ethiopia	11	38	2	12	0	0	1	1			1	0
Fiji	85	135	20	68	0	3	3	13	0	0	16	10
Finland	92	100	76	116	11	27	34	70	11	11	65	76
France	100	106	56	111	14	25	30	51	16	12	45	57
French Polynesia		115		86				2			2	3

TABLE A, *continued*

Country	Primary 1965	Primary 1995	Secondary 1965	Secondary 1995	Tertiary 1965	Tertiary 1975	Tertiary 1985	Tertiary 1995	Tertiary 1965 Male	Tertiary 1965 Female	Tertiary 1995 Male	Tertiary 1995 Female
Gabon	100		11		0	2	5	8			11	5
Gambia, The	21	77	6	25	0	0	0	2	0	0	2	1
Georgia		82		73				38			35	41
Germany	100	103	45	102	9	25	30	44	13	4	47	41
Ghana	69	76	13	32	1	1	2	1	1	0	2	1
Greece	100	94	49	96	10	18	26	43	13	6	43	42
Guam		69		185				66			58	74
Guatemala	50	84	8	25	2	4	8	8	4	1	12	4
Guinea	32	48	5	12	0	3	2	1			2	0
Guinea-Bissau	26	68	2	11	0	0	0		0	0		
Guyana	100	95	53	75	1	4	2	10	1	0	10	9
Haiti	50	51	5	24	1	1	1	1	1	0	2	1
Honduras	80	110	10	32	2	5	10	11	2	1	12	10
Hong Kong, China	100	96	29	75	5	10	13	26	6	5	28	23
Hungary	100	104	60	99			16	24	15	10	22	26
Iceland	98	98	72	104	8	16	22	36	11	5	29	42
India	74	100	27	49	5	9	9	7	4	1	8	5
Indonesia	72	115	12	50	3	2	7	11	3	1	15	8
Iran, Islamic Rep. of	47	94	28	75	2	5	5	17	2	1	21	13
Iraq	74	85	28	42	4	9	12	11	6	2	14	9
Ireland	100	103	51	115	12	19	24	39	16	8	37	40
Israel	95	99	48	89	20	25	34	41	22	18	39	44
Italy	100	99	47	88	11	26	24	41	14	7	38	45
Jamaica	100	110	51	70	3	7	4	8	4	3	8	7
Japan	100	102	82	103	13	25	29	41	20	6	45	38
Jordan	95		38		2	9		17	2	1	18	17
Kazakhstan		96		83				33			29	37
Kenya	54	85	4	24	0	1	1	2	1	0	2	1
Korea, Rep. of	100	95	35	101	6	10	34	52	9	3	66	38
Kuwait	100	73	52	64	0	9	15	25	0	0	22	28
Kyrgyz Republic		107		81				12			12	13
Lao PDR		102		28				2			2	1
Latvia		89		85				26			22	30
Lebanon		109		81				27			27	27
Lesotho	94	100	4	29	0	1	2	2	1	0	2	3
Liberia	41	33	5	15	1	2	3	3	1	0	5	2
Libya		114		102				20			20	20
Lithuania		96		84				28			23	34
Luxembourg	100		33		3	2	3	3			4	2
Macao								27			28	25
Macedonia, FYR		89		57				18			16	20
Madagascar	65	73	8	13	1	1	4	2			2	2
Malawi	44	135	2	16	0	1	1	1	0	0	1	0
Malaysia	90	92	28	61	2	3	6	11	3	1	12	10
Maldives		133		58								
Mali	24	34	4	10	0	1	1	1	0	0	1	0
Malta	100	109	26	85	5	5	6	24	7	3	24	24
Mauritania	13	79	1	16	0	0	3	4			6	1
Mauritius	100	107	26	62	0	1	1	7	0	0	7	7
Mexico	92	115	17	61	4	11	16	15	6	1	16	14
Moldova		94		80				25			22	28
Mongolia		88		59				15			9	21
Morocco	57	83	11	39	1	3	8	11			13	9
Mozambique	37	60	3	7	0	0	0	0	0	0	1	0
Myanmar	71	101	15	32	1	2		6	2	1	4	7

TABLE A, *continued*

Country	Primary 1965	Primary 1995	Secondary 1965	Secondary 1995	Tertiary 1965	Tertiary 1975	Tertiary 1985	Tertiary 1995	Tertiary 1965 Male	Tertiary 1965 Female	Tertiary 1995 Male	Tertiary 1995 Female
Namibia		133		62				8			6	10
Nepal	20	108	5	38	1	2	5	5	2	0	7	2
Netherlands	100	107	61	137	17	26	32	49	24	9	50	47
New Caledonia		123		102				5			6	4
New Zealand	100	104	75	117	15	26	34	58	18	11	51	66
Nicaragua	69	110	14	47	2	8	10	12	4	1	12	12
Niger	11	29	1	7	0	0	1	1	0	0	1	0
Nigeria	32	88	5	32	0	1	3	4			6	2
Norway	97	99	64	117	11	22	30	59	14	8	51	66
Oman		80		67	0	0	1	5			6	5
Pakistan	40	79	12	30	2	2	5	3	3	1	4	3
Panama	100	104	34	68	7	17	26	30	7	7	24	36
Papua New Guinea	44	80	4	14	0	3	2	3	0	0	4	2
Paraguay	100	111	13	40	4	7	9	11	4	3	11	12
Peru	99	123	25	70	8	15	24	31	11	6	37	25
Philippines	100	116	41	79	19	18	38	30	17	21	25	34
Poland	100	96	48	98	13	17	17	25	19	16	21	29
Portugal	84	132	42	111	5	11	12	37	7	4	32	43
Puerto Rico								42			35	49
Qatar		86		80				28			15	42
Reunion												
Romania		100		78				18			19	18
Russian Federation		111		86				42			38	47
Rwanda	53	97	2	14	0	0	0	1	0	0	0	1
Samoa		103										
Saudi Arabia	24	78	4	58	1	4	12	16			16	15
Senegal	40	65	7	16	1	2	2	3	2	0	5	2
Seychelles												
Sierra Leone	29	53	5	17	0	1	1	2	1	0	3	1
Singapore	100	95	45	73	10	9	12	34	13	7	37	31
Slovak Republic		103		94				20			20	21
Slovenia		103		91				33			28	39
Solomon Islands		100		18								
Somalia	10	9	2	5	0	1	3	2			4	1
South Africa	90	117	15	84	4	6		17	6	2	18	17
Spain	100	106	38	121	6	20	29	49	9	3	45	53
Sri Lanka	93	113	35	75	2	1	4	5	2	1	6	4
St. Kitts and Nevis												
St. Lucia												
St. Vincent and the Grenadines												
Sudan	29	52	4	19	1	2	2	4	1	0	5	3
Suriname	100		28			6	7	13			12	14
Swaziland	74	126	8	66	0	3	4	4	0	0	4	4
Sweden	95	106	62	136	13	29	31	46	15	11	40	52
Switzerland	87		37		8	14	21	33	13	3	41	25
Syrian Arab Republic	78	101	28	43	8	12	18	15	13	3	18	13
Tajikistan		91		79				20			26	14
Tanzania	32	67	2	5	0	0	0	1	0	0	1	0
Thailand	78	87	14	55	2	4	20	20	2	1	19	22
Togo	55	119	5	27	0	1	2	3	0	0	6	1
Trinidad and Tobago	93	96	36	72	2	5	4	8	3	2	8	7
Tunisia	91	116	16	61	2	4	6	13	3	1	14	12
Turkey	100	108	16	59	4	9	10	18	6	2	22	14
Turkmenistan		110		115				20			19	21
Uganda	67	73	4	12	0	1	1	2	1	0	2	1

TABLE A, *continued*

Country	Primary 1965	Primary 1995	Secondary 1965	Secondary 1995	Tertiary 1965	Tertiary 1975	Tertiary 1985	Tertiary 1995	Tertiary 1965 Male	Tertiary 1965 Female	Tertiary 1995 Male	Tertiary 1995 Female
Ukraine		88		92				42			36	47
United Arab Emirates		91		78	0	0	8	11		0	5	19
United Kingdom	92	116	66	133	12	19	22	50	17	7	47	52
United States	100	102	90	97	40	57	58	81	49	31	71	92
Uruguay	100	111	44	82	8	16	24	28	10	7	24	33
Uzbekistan		78		93				35			33	37
Vanuatu		105		21								
Venezuela	94	90	27	35	7	18	26	26	9	5	25	27
Vietnam		114						4			6	3
Yemen, Rep. of	9	73	0	31	0	1	2	4	0	0	7	1
Yugoslavia, FR (Serb./Mont.)	100	72	65	65	13	20	19	21	17	9	19	23
Zambia	53	89	7	28	0	2	1	3	0	0	4	2
Zimbabwe	100	116	6	47	0	2	3	6	0	0	9	4
World	82	102	32	63	9	14	13	18	11	6	18	18
Low and middle income	76	102	21	55	4	7	7	10	5	2	11	9
Sub-Saharan Africa	45	74	5	25	1	1	2	3	1	0	5	2
East Asia and Pacific	87	115	23	64	5	5	4	7	5	4	9	6
South Asia	67	95	24	44	4	7	8	6	3	1	8	4
Europe and Central Asia	100	101	39	83	9	14	13	32	13	9	29	34
Latin America and the Caribbean	94	112	19	55	4	13	16	18	6	3	18	18
Middle East and N. Africa	62	94	20	62	3	7	11	15	6	2	18	12
High income	99	103	67	106	20	33	37	58	25	14	55	61

Source: Columns 1, 3, 5–7, 9, and 10: Barro and Lee 1994; columns 2, 4, 8, 11, and 12: UNESCO 1999a.

TABLE B. TERTIARY ENROLLMENT DATA

Country	Number of Tertiary Students					Number of Tertiary Students per 100,000 Inhabitants			
	1975	1980	1985 or closest yr.	1990	1995 or LYA**	1980	1985 or closest yr.	1990	1995 or LYA**
Afghanistan	12,256	20,279	22,306	24,333	26,360	142		147	
Albania		14,568	21,995	22,059	30,185	545	1,080	679	899
Algeria	41,847	79,351	132,057	285,930	347,410	530	798	1,146	1,236
Angola		2,333	5,034	6,534	8,784	33		71	
Argentina	596,736	491,473	846,145	1,008,231	1,069,617	1,741	2,792	3,293	3,117
Armenia		109,900	102,700	114,300	39,592	1,890	3,076	2,030	1,090
Australia	274,738	323,716	370,048	485,075	964,998	2,203	2,366	2,839	5,401
Austria	96,736	136,774	173,215	205,767	238,981	1,812	2,292	2,668	2,970
Azerbaijan		186,024	182,145	163,901	118,105	1,720	2,731	1,470	1,568
Bahamas, The		4,093	4,531	5,305	6,079	1,949		2,192	
Bahrain	703	1,908	4,180	6,868	7,676	550	1,011	1,365	1,445
Bangladesh		240,181	461,073	681,965	902,857	272		382	
Barbados		4,033	5,227	6,651	3,064	1,620	2,075	1,657	2,572
Belarus	314,603	339,800	342,400	335,284	313,800	1,760	3,425	1,700	3,031
Belgium	159,660	196,153	247,499	276,248	352,630	2,111	2,511	2,725	3,494
Belize		107,000	104,493	101,986	99,483				
Benin	2,118	4,822	9,063	10,873	11,227	139	225	235	208
Bermuda		608							
Bolivia	49,850	60,900	88,175	102,001	120,756	1,494		1,975	
Botswana	469	1,078	1,938	2,957	7,920	120	180	299	546
Brazil	1,089,808	1,409,243	1,451,191	1,540,080	1,716,263	1,162	1,052	1,074	1,094
Brunei		143	601	1,163	1,270	74	262	395	518
Bulgaria	128,593	101,359	113,795	188,479	250,336	1,144	1,270	2,096	2,942
Burkina Faso	1,067	1,644	4,085	5,425	9,388	24	52	60	90
Burundi	1,002	1,879	2,783	3,592	4,256	45	59	65	74
Cambodia		601	2,213	6,659	11,652				119
Cameroon		11,686	21,438	33,177	47,665	135		288	
Canada	1,079,960	1,172,750	1,639,410	1,916,801	2,011,485	4,035	6,320	5,102	6,984
Central African Republic	669	1,719	2,651	3,840	3,450	74		119	
Chad	547	1,470	1,643	2,242	3,446		38	70	54
Chile	149,647	145,497	197,437	261,800	342,788	1,305	1,639	1,938	2,412
China	500,993	1,662,796	3,515,485	3,822,371	5,621,543	117	328	186	461
Colombia	176,098	271,630	391,490	487,448	588,322	1,024	1,331	1,496	1,643
Comoros		316	281	248	348				
Congo, Dem. Rep. of	24,853	28,493	40,878	80,233	93,266	105	129	176	212
Congo, Rep. of	3,249	7,255	10,684	10,671	13,806	435	555	479	582
Costa Rica	33,239	55,593	63,771	74,681	78,819	2,434	2,414	2,461	2,919
Côte d'Ivoire	7,174	19,633	21,650	23,073	55,000	240	219		413
Croatia		64,966	55,886	72,342	86,357		1,250		1,917
Cuba	82,688	151,733	235,224	242,434	122,346	1,568	2,325	2,285	1,116
Cyprus	602	1,940	3,134	6,554	8,874	308	575		
Czech Republic	90,649	118,026	107,098	118,194	191,604		1,039		1,867
Denmark	110,271	106,241	116,319	142,968	166,545	2,074	2,275	2,625	3,188
Djibouti			53		130		10		22
Dominican Republic		42,400	123,748	123,724	176,995		1,941		2,223
Ecuador	170,173	269,775	280,594	206,541	174,924	3,321		1,950	
Egypt, Arab Rep. of	480,016	715,701	854,584	628,233	850,051	1,751	1,717	1,698	1,900
El Salvador	28,281	16,838	70,499	78,211	114,998	372	1,508	1,512	2,031
Eritrea					3,020				95
Estonia		25,500	24,680	25,900	39,726	1,723	1,625	1,636	2,670

TABLE B, *continued*

Country	Number of Tertiary Students					Number of Tertiary Students per 100,000 Inhabitants			
	1975	1980	1985 or closest yr.	1990	1995 or LYA**	1980	1985 or closest yr.	1990	1995 or LYA**
Ethiopia		14,368	27,338	34,076	35,027	37	66	68	62
Fiji	1,653	1,666	2,313	3,509		263		1,080	
Finland	114,272	123,165	127,976	165,714	213,995	2,577	2,611	3,326	4,190
France	1,038,576	1,076,717	1,278,581	1,698,938	2,091,688	1,998	2,318	2,995	3,600
French Polynesia		27							
Gabon	1,014	4,031	4,089	4,031	3,972	216		375	
Gambia, The					1,591				148
Georgia		140,578	144,400	148,391	155,033	1,680	2,731	1,900	2,845
Germany				2,048,627	2,144,169		2,581		2,628
Ghana	9,079	7,951	8,324	9,242	10,170	144		126	
Greece	117,246	121,116	181,901	283,415	329,185	1,256	1,831	1,927	3,149
Guam	3,800	3,217	5,134	7,052	8,969				
Guatemala	22,881	50,890	48,283	64,103	80,228	736	741		755
Guinea	12,411	18,270	8,801	5,366	7,722	410	176	122	105
Guinea-Bissau									
Guyana	2,852	2,465	2,328	4,665	7,680	325	294	588	926
Haiti	2,881	4,671	6,288	7,905	9,522	87			
Honduras	11,907	25,825	36,620	43,117	54,106	705	875	854	985
Hong Kong, China	44,482	38,153	76,844	85,214	97,392	1,201	1,425		1,635
Hungary	107,555	101,166	99,344	102,387	179,563	945	939	970	1,777
Iceland	2,970	3,633	4,724	5,225	7,483	1,593	1,957	2,049	2,756
India	3,043,865	3,545,318	4,470,844	4,950,974	5,695,780	515	582		613
Indonesia	278,200	543,175	1,277,684	1,590,593	2,303,469	367	749	838	1,167
Iran, Islamic Rep. of	151,905	184,442	239,300	312,076	1,048,093	317	469	858	1,533
Iraq	86,111	106,709	169,665	209,818	249,971	820		1,240	
Ireland	46,174	54,746	70,301	90,296	128,284	1,610	1,979	2,578	3,618
Israel		97,097	116,062	134,885	198,766	2,504	2,742	2,790	3,598
Italy	976,712	1,117,742	1,185,304	1,452,286	1,775,186	1,981	2,088	2,519	3,103
Jamaica	3,963	13,999	10,969	16,018	8,191	656	475	662	770
Japan	2,248,903	2,412,117	2,347,463	2,683,035	3,917,709	2,065	1,943	2,328	3,139
Jordan	11,873	36,549	53,753	80,442	99,020	1,713		2,230	
Kazakhstan		525,400	551,000	537,441	472,000	1,730	3,481	1,710	2,807
Kenya		12,986	21,756	31,287	67,371	78		140	
Korea, Rep. of	318,683	647,505	1,455,759	1,691,429	2,225,092	1,698	3,568	3,899	4,974
Kuwait	8,104	13,630	23,678	20,787	28,705	991	1,377	1,244	2,247
Kyrgyz Republic		64,595	71,330	57,563	49,744	1,510	1,777	1,330	1,115
Lao PDR		1,408	5,382	4,730	12,732	44	150	116	253
Latvia		47,230	43,914	45,953	44,064	1,863	1,692	1,712	1,737
Lebanon		79,073	79,500	82,497	81,588	2,963	2,980	3,071	2,712
Lesotho	529	1,188	1,771	2,029	4,384	141	113	263	216
Liberia	2,404	4,900	4,889	4,878	4,847	208		218	
Libya	13,427	20,166	30,000	50,471	106,541	663		1,548	
Lithuania		70,995	96,500	88,668	75,559	2,063	2,621	1,758	2,023
Luxembourg	483	748	759			207			
Macao		7,930	7,718	7,425	7,485				1,700
Macedonia, FYR	36,049	46,281	38,065	26,515	29,583		1,979		1,372
Madagascar	8,385	22,632	38,310	35,824	28,814	257	359	298	194
Malawi	1,903	2,591	3,057	4,829	5,561	56	42	63	58
Malaysia		57,650	93,249	121,412	191,290	419	595	679	971
Maldives									

TABLE B, *continued*

Country	Number of Tertiary Students					Number of Tertiary Students per 100,000 Inhabitants			
	1975	1980	1985 or closest yr.	1990	1995 or LYA**	1980	1985 or closest yr.	1990	1995 or LYA**
Mali	2,936	1,631	6,768	6,703	6,687	64		73	
Malta	1,425	947	1,474	3,123	5,805	292	428	791	1,595
Mauritania		5,378	4,526	5,339	8,496		256	281	374
Mauritius	1,096	1,038	1,161	3,485	6,799	107	114	208	609
Mexico	562,056	929,865	1,207,779	1,310,835	1,420,461	1,387	1,600	1,552	1,586
Moldova		110,200	113,800	104,800	87,700	1,270	2,700	1,250	1,976
Mongolia	9,861	34,543	40,099	31,434	38,643	2,234	2,101	1,416	1,569
Morocco	45,322	112,405	181,087	255,667	294,502	580	837	958	1,132
Mozambique		1,000	1,442	3,698	6,639	8	11	16	41
Myanmar	56,083	163,197	179,366	196,052	250,000	478	478	516	564
Namibia		558	1,523	4,157	11,344			280	738
Nepal	23,504	34,094	54,452	93,753	102,018	259	424	549	501
Netherlands	288,026	360,033	404,866	478,869	491,748	2,545	2,794	2,945	3,176
New Caledonia	178	438	761						
New Zealand	66,178	76,643	95,793	111,504	163,923	2,462	2,950	3,287	4,603
Nicaragua	18,282	35,268	29,001	30,733	50,769	1,259	905	836	1,231
Niger	541	1,435	2,863	3,684	5,867	26		60	
Nigeria	44,964	150,072	266,679	335,824	404,969	191		320	
Norway	66,628	79,117	94,658	142,521	180,383	1,936	2,279	3,357	4,164
Oman		18	990	6,208	9,664	2	670	391	438
Pakistan	127,932		267,742	336,689	371,162	182		266	
Panama	26,289	40,369	55,303	53,235	76,839	2,064	2,552	2,181	2,921
Papua New Guinea		5,040	5,068	6,397	13,663	163	147		318
Paraguay	18,302	26,915	32,090	32,884	40,913	855	889	769	1,031
Peru	195,641	306,353	452,462	681,801	755,929	1,771	2,321	3,450	3,268
Philippines	769,749	1,276,016	1,402,000	1,709,486	2,022,106	2,621	2,565	2,738	2,981
Poland	575,499	589,134	454,190	544,893	747,638	1,656	1,221	1,427	1,946
Portugal	79,702	92,152	129,277	185,762	300,573	944	1,305	1,882	3,060
Puerto Rico	97,517	131,184	142,407	153,680	164,854				
Qatar	779	2,269	5,344	6,485	8,271	991	1,494	1,559	1,509
Reunion									
Romania	164,567	192,769	159,798	192,810	336,141	868	703	711	1,479
Russian Federation	5,500,000	5,700,000	5,444,000	5,100,000	4,458,363	2,190	3,768	1,900	2,998
Rwanda	1,108	1,243	1,987	3,389	4,791	24		50	
Samoa	249	976	758	900	1,042				
Saudi Arabia	26,437	62,074	113,529	153,967	251,945	662	898	1,035	1,380
Senegal		13,626	13,354	18,689	24,081	246	209	253	297
Seychelles		144							
Sierra Leone	1,701	2,166	5,690	4,742	3,794	66		114	
Singapore	22,607	23,256	39,913	55,672	83,914	963	1,474		2,522
Slovak Republic		77,191	66,002	72,215	91,553		1,247		1,715
Slovenia		27,707	29,601	33,565	47,908		1,574		2,489
Solomon Islands									
Somalia	2,040	2,900	8,221	13,543	20,994	45			
South Africa		207,620		439,007	617,897				1,524
Spain	540,238	697,789	935,126	1,222,089	1,591,863	1,859	2,431	3,007	4,017
Sri Lanka	15,426	42,694	59,377	55,190	63,660	288	370	488	474
St. Kitts and Nevis		99	212	325	394				
St. Lucia		301	367	618	2,760				
St. Vincent and the Grenadines			736	677	618				

TABLE B, *continued*

Country	Number of Tertiary Students					Number of Tertiary Students per 100,000 Inhabitants			
	1975	1980	1985 or closest yr.	1990	1995 or LYA**	1980	1985 or closest yr.	1990	1995 or LYA**
Sudan	21,342	28,788	37,367	60,134	82,901	154		245	
Suriname		2,378	2,751	3,994	4,804	676		1,023	
Swaziland	1,012	1,875	2,732	3,198	3,497	332	421	426	408
Sweden	162,640	171,356	176,589	192,611	261,209	2,062	2,115	2,248	2,972
Switzerland	64,720	85,127	110,111	137,486	148,024	1,347	1,685	2,048	2,066
Syrian Arab Republic	73,660	140,180	179,473	221,628	215,734	1,611	1,726	1,740	1,559
Tajikistan		96,900	95,247	109,653	108,203	1,420	2,086	1,280	1,890
Tanzania	3,064	5,000	4,863	5,058	12,776	22	22	21	43
Thailand	130,965	361,400	1,026,952	952,012	1,220,481	1,284	2,009	1,763	2,096
Togo	2,353	4,750	5,230	8,969	11,639	182	173	226	285
Trinidad and Tobago	4,940	5,649	6,582	7,249	5,348	522	559	591	730
Tunisia	20,505	31,827	41,594	68,535	112,634	499	567	851	1,253
Turkey	327,082	246,183	469,992	749,921	1,174,299	554	934	1,339	1,960
Turkmenistan		69,800	75,800	76,000	76,200	1,240		1,130	
Uganda	5,474	5,856	10,103	17,578	30,266	45	68	100	154
Ukraine	1,570,100	1,683,500	1,662,000	1,651,700	1,541,000	1,760	3,263	1,700	2,977
United Arab Emirates		2,861	7,772	10,196	15,789	282	501	642	801
United Kingdom	732,947	827,146	1,032,491	1,258,188	1,820,843	1,468	1,824	2,170	3,135
United States	11,184,859	12,096,895	12,247,055	13,710,150	14,261,778	5,311	5,064	5,591	5,339
Uruguay	32,627	36,298	53,955	71,612	79,691	1,338		2,315	2,488
Uzbekistan		515,800	567,200	602,700	691,450	1,720		1,650	
Vanuatu									
Venezuela	213,542	307,133	443,064	550,030	551,912	2,044		2,847	
Vietnam	80,323	114,701	121,159	129,600	297,900	214	202		404
Yemen, Rep. of		7,811	26,673	45,536	65,675				419
Yugoslavia, FR (Serb./Mont.)					159,512				1,556
Zambia	8,403	3,425	14,492	15,343	10,489	131	221	189	241
Zimbabwe	8,479	8,339	30,843	49,361	45,593	117	368	496	626
World	40,267,422	50,758,289	58,394,175	68,275,579	80,459,713	1,021	1,335	1,318	1,531
Low and middle income	18,986,254	26,929,371	33,645,255	37,313,806	44,155,455	602	879	761	980
Sub-Saharan Africa	181,386	618,089	660,360	1,316,906	1,750,684	117	124	181	339
East Asia and Pacific	1,828,765	4,224,145	7,673,191	8,575,155	11,984,521	293	521	441	704
South Asia	3,222,983	3,882,888	5,335,794	6,142,904	7,161,837	445	574	338	608
Europe and Central Asia	9,209,689	11,649,860	11,453,615	11,579,161	11,547,310	1,656	2,539	1,608	2,436
Latin America and the Caribbean	3,590,200	4,945,840	6,389,251	7,267,699	7,923,878	1,346	1,493	1,706	1,638
Middle East and N. Africa	953,231	1,608,549	2,133,044	2,431,981	3,787,225	943	1,053	1,251	1,465
High income	21,281,168	23,828,918	24,748,920	30,961,773	36,304,258	3,033	3,197	3,701	4,071

**LYA Last year available.

Source: Column 1: UNESCO 1999a; columns 2 and 4: UNESCO 1999a, supplemented by Bloom and Rivera-Batiz 1999; columns 3 and 5: UNESCO 1998a, supplemented by Bloom and Rivera-Batiz 1999; columns 6 and 8: UNESCO 1993; columns 7 and 9: UNESCO 1998a.

TABLE C. ATTAINMENT RATES (%, population over 25)

Country	Primary Attained		Secondary Attained		Tertiary Attained				Average Years of Schooling in Population over 25	
	1965	1990	1965	1990	1965	1975	1985	1995	1965	1990
Afghanistan	4	9	3	3	3	2	3	2	0.9	1.0
Albania								7		
Algeria	10	32	2	9	0	1	2	5	0.6	2.8
Angola								1		
Argentina	72	57	12	25	4	6	8	15	5.2	7.8
Armenia								23		
Australia	37	27	57	48	5	21	22	24	8.9	10.1
Austria	86	43	8	47	3	4	6	12	4.0	7.4
Azerbaijan								18		
Bahamas, The										
Bahrain	9	26	6	25	3	3	3	11	1.4	4.6
Bangladesh	11	23	6	14	1	1	2	3	0.9	2.2
Barbados	81	48	18	42	1	2	6	10	5.4	8.2
Belarus								24		
Belgium	64	48	29	37	5	7	11	16	7.8	8.8
Belize								14		
Benin		13	1	5	0	0	1	2		1.3
Bermuda										
Bolivia	22	39	26	11	4	5	8	12	4.2	4.1
Botswana	25	41	2	7	0	1	1	2	1.3	2.6
Brazil	44	66	11	5	2	4	6	8	2.8	3.6
Brunei										
Bulgaria	63	44	15	36	5	7	9	17	6.4	9.3
Burkina Faso								0		
Burundi								1		
Cambodia										
Cameroon	20	38	5	7	0	0	1	2	1.3	2.3
Canada	47	16	36	62	14	31	19	29	7.8	10.3
Central African Republic	5	22	2	4	0	0	0	1	0.4	1.3
Chad								1		
Chile	57	57	21	25	2	5	8	12	4.7	6.2
China		34		34	1	1	1	2		5.2
Colombia	49	52	10	17	2	3	6	9	2.8	4.3
Comoros								0		
Congo, Dem. Rep. of	17	32	1	10	0	0	1	1	0.7	2.2
Congo, Rep. of		21	13	23	3	2	3	4		3.9
Costa Rica	69	62	8	11	3	6	12	16	3.8	5.4
Côte d'Ivoire								8		
Croatia								8		
Cuba	61	57	5	27	2	3	7	12	3.7	6.6
Cyprus	59	41	15	40	1	9	14	13	4.3	7.8
Czech Republic								9		
Denmark	50	39	34	42	16	16	19	21	10.0	11.2
Djibouti								0		
Dominican Republic	48	36	3	11	1	3	6	11	2.2	3.8
Ecuador	52	49	7	9	2	3	14	18	2.9	5.6
Egypt, Arab Rep. of		19		16	2	3	5	9		3.6
El Salvador	33	54	4	5	1	2	3	8	1.7	3.4
Eritrea										
Estonia								15		

TABLE C, *continued*

Country	Primary Attained		Secondary Attained		Tertiary Attained				Average Years of Schooling in Population over 25	
	1965	1990	1965	1990	1965	1975	1985	1995	1965	1990
Ethiopia								1		
Fiji	64	54	8	33	5	3	5	6	4.7	7.5
Finland	84	49	11	35	5	7	14	19	7.7	9.8
France	88	58	10	28	3	5	11	16	4.8	6.9
French Polynesia										
Gabon								3		
Gambia, The		6	3	6	0	0	0			0.9
Georgia								23		
Germany	81	65	16	22	2	6	8	15	7.9	8.8
Ghana	14	24	2	17	1	1	1	1	0.8	2.8
Greece	69	57	10	29	3	5	9	11	5.0	7.7
Guam										
Guatemala	27	37	4	6	1	1	4	5	1.4	2.6
Guinea								2		
Guinea-Bissau										
Guyana	82	57	5	30	0	1	2	3	3.7	5.4
Haiti	6	28	4	10	0	0	1	1	0.7	2.2
Honduras	34	52	3	11	1	1	3	6	1.7	3.7
Hong Kong, China	40	30	18	43	5	4	8	14	4.9	8.4
Hungary	86	63	8	26	4	6	8	11	6.9	8.4
Iceland	82	53	13	35	4	6	9	13	5.9	8.0
India	21	20	3	14	0	2	4	5	1.5	3.6
Indonesia	25	54	2	12	0	1	1	4	1.3	3.9
Iran, Islamic Rep. of	7	18	3	19	1	2	3	5	0.8	3.3
Iraq	3	22	2	13	1	2	5	8	0.4	3.1
Ireland	65	40	27	44	5	6	10	14	6.5	8.2
Israel	43	28	27	34	10	16	24	27	6.8	9.0
Italy	72	44	14	32	3	4	7	12	4.8	6.2
Jamaica	78	64	5	29	1	2	3	4	2.5	4.5
Japan	54	34	37	45	7	7	16	22	7.1	9.2
Jordan	16	17	8	18	1	1	11	19	1.7	5.2
Kazakhstan								16		
Kenya	20	45	2	7	0	1	1	1	1.2	2.8
Korea, Rep. of	35	22	18	54	4	7	12	19	4.4	9.3
Kuwait	36	6	12	34	3	7	13	13	2.7	5.7
Kyrgyz Republic								15		
Lao PDR								1		
Latvia								15		
Lebanon								21		
Lesotho	57	59	2	6	0	0	1	1	2.7	3.3
Liberia	8	17	2	11	1	2	2	2	0.6	1.9
Libya	15	27	1	20	0	1	3	7	0.6	3.9
Lithuania								15		
Luxembourg										
Macao								9		
Macedonia, FYR								16		
Madagascar								2		
Malawi	32	39	0	4	0	0	0	1	1.7	2.4
Malaysia	39	45	8	27	1	2	2	4	2.7	5.6
Maldives										

Country	Primary Attained		Secondary Attained		Tertiary Attained				Average Years of Schooling in Population over 25	
	1965	1990	1965	1990	1965	1975	1985	1995	1965	1990
Mali	3	8	0	3	0	0	0	1	0.2	0.8
Malta	58	44	17	31	2	3	3	5	5.1	6.6
Mauritania								2		
Mauritius	47	49	8	31	1	2	3	2	2.8	5.2
Mexico	47	49	4	23	2	3	7	10	2.5	5.9
Moldova								14		
Mongolia								10		
Morocco								6		
Mozambique	8	26	1	1	0	0	0	0	0.3	0.7
Myanmar	11	32	8	14	1	0	2	3	0.9	2.2
Namibia										
Nepal	0	9	1	5	0	0	2	3	0.1	1.0
Netherlands	82	34	14	46	3	9	14	19	5.6	8.6
New Caledonia										
New Zealand	40	37	54	24	5	20	30	39	9.4	11.2
Nicaragua	33	44	3	6	4	5	8	8	2.0	3.3
Niger	4	10	0	1	0	0	0	0	0.2	0.6
Nigeria								2		
Norway	77	50	16	32	2	9	14	19	5.6	7.9
Oman								1		
Pakistan	12	10	4	14	0	3	2	3	0.9	2.3
Panama	55	42	15	29	3	5	11	18	4.1	7.6
Papua New Guinea	15	24	5	6	0	0	1	1	1.0	1.7
Paraguay	67	67	6	14	1	3	5	6	3.3	4.7
Peru	45	46	9	17	3	6	12	17	3.0	5.5
Philippines	52	54	10	15	8	12	18	23	3.9	6.7
Poland	67	43	22	48	4	7	8	9	7.1	9.6
Portugal	50	59	3	11	1	2	5	8	2.2	3.6
Puerto Rico								34		
Qatar								17		
Reunion	45		8		1	1	1		2.3	
Romania	67	24	16	63	3	5	6	8	5.6	9.2
Russian Federation								18		
Rwanda		35	2	2	0	0	0	0		1.5
Samoa										
Saudi Arabia								7		
Senegal	28	31	2	4	1	1	1	2	1.4	1.9
Seychelles										
Sierra Leone	4	13	2	5	0	0	1	1	0.5	1.3
Singapore	26	35	22	31	1	3	4	7	3.5	5.5
Slovak Republic								10		
Slovenia								11		
Solomon Islands										
Somalia										
South Africa	27	47	24	23	1	4	2	4	3.8	4.8
Spain	64	64	5	21	4	4	7	13	3.8	6.3
Sri Lanka	48	46	20	36	0	2	1	2	3.6	5.4
St. Kitts and Nevis										
St. Lucia										
St. Vincent and the Grenadines										

TABLE C, *continued*

Country	Primary Attained		Secondary Attained		Tertiary Attained				Average Years of Schooling in Population over 25	
	1965	1990	1965	1990	1965	1975	1985	1995	1965	1990
Sudan	10	21	1	6	0	0	1	1	0.3	1.2
Suriname										
Swaziland	21	43	6	11	0	0	1	2	1.7	3.5
Sweden	57	35	35	44	8	12	17	20	7.7	9.5
Switzerland	69	29	22	52	9	9	12	14	6.9	8.9
Syrian Arab Republic	24	35	3	14	1	3	8	12	1.3	4.4
Tajikistan								13		
Tanzania								0		
Thailand	50	65	5	5	1	2	5	10	3.1	5.2
Togo	7	23	1	13	0	0	2	2	0.4	2.5
Trinidad and Tobago	75	62	12	29	1	2	3	4	4.4	6.3
Tunisia	7	26	3	13	1	1	3	4	0.7	3.0
Turkey	33	41	6	12	1	2	4	7	2.1	3.4
Turkmenistan								19		
Uganda	27	31	2	3	0	0	0	1	1.1	1.4
Ukraine								24		
United Arab Emirates						6		6		
United Kingdom	69	44	27	39	3	11	13	16	7.2	8.7
United States	36	9	44	44	18	25	34	49	9.3	12.0
Uruguay	70	56	10	27	5	6	8	14	4.8	6.7
Uzbekistan								23		
Vanuatu										
Venezuela	44	55	5	12	2	5	10	15	2.4	4.9
Vietnam								3		
Yemen, Rep. of								2		
Yugoslavia, FR (Serb./Mont.)	59	42	8	31	3	6	9	11	4.8	7.2
Zambia	32	50	1	12	0	1	1	1	1.8	4.1
Zimbabwe	46	56	2	4	0	1	1	2	1.6	2.3
World	42	34	15	26	3	5	7	10	4.2	5.7
Low and middle income	30	34	6	22	1	2	3	6	2.1	4.4
Sub-Saharan Africa	19	33	5	10	0	1	1	2	1.4	2.5
East Asia and Pacific	31	38	4	30	1	1	2	3	2.0	5.1
South Asia	19	20	3	14	0	2	3	4	1.4	3.3
Europe and Central Asia	60	41	14	35	3	5	6	16	5.4	7.3
Latin America and the Caribbean	49	56	9	14	2	4	7	11	3.1	4.8
Middle East and N. Africa	9	22	3	16	1	2	4	7	0.8	3.4
High income	58	34	28	39	8	13	18	26	7.1	9.4

Source: Columns 1 through 7: Barro and Lee 1996; column 8: Bloom and Rivera-Batiz 1999; columns 9 and 10: Barro and Lee 1996.

TABLE D. PUBLIC EXPENDITURE ON EDUCATION AS A WHOLE

Country	% of GNP 1970	% of Gov't Spending 1970	% of GNP 1980	% of Gov't Spending 1980	% of GNP 1990	% of Gov't Spending 1990	% of GNP 1995	% of Gov't Spending 1995
Afghanistan	1.1		2.0	12.7				
Albania				10.3	5.8			
Algeria	7.9	31.6	7.8	24.3	5.5	21.1	5.8	14.7
Angola					4.9	10.7		
Argentina		9.1	2.7	15.1	1.1	10.9	3.3	11.6
Armenia					7.3	20.5		
Australia	4.1	13.3	5.5	14.8	5.4	14.8		
Austria	4.5	8.1	5.5	8.0	5.4	7.6	5.7	10.6
Azerbaijan					7.0	23.5	2.9	17.5
Bahamas, The	4.8	19.4			4.3	17.8		
Bahrain		20.0	2.9	9.4	5.0	14.6	4.8	12.8
Bangladesh			1.5	7.8	2.0	10.3		
Barbados	5.8	21.2	6.5	20.5	7.9	22.2		
Belarus		18.7			4.9		5.6	17.1
Belgium			6.0	16.3	5.1		3.1	5.8
Belize	3.8		2.4	14.5	4.8	18.5	5.3	19.6
Benin							3.2	15.2
Bermuda	3.6	18.8	4.0		3.3	14.5		
Bolivia	3.4	28.4	4.4	25.3	2.7		6.6	
Botswana	4.7		6.0	16.0	6.9	17.0	8.6	15.8
Brazil	2.9	10.6	3.6				5.5	
Brunei		13.9		11.8	2.5			
Bulgaria		9.1	4.5		5.6		4.0	
Burkina Faso			2.2	19.8	2.7		1.4	
Burundi					3.4	16.7	4.1	
Cambodia	5.8	23.5						
Cameroon	3.4	19.6	3.6	20.3	3.5	19.6		
Canada	8.7	24.1	6.9	16.3	6.8	14.2		
Central African Republic					2.2			
Chad								
Chile	5.1	22.0	4.6	11.9	2.7	10.4	3.0	14.0
China	1.2	4.3	2.5	9.3	2.3	12.8	2.3	
Colombia	1.9	13.6	2.4	19.2	2.6	16.0	4.0	18.6
Comoros								
Congo, Dem. Rep. of			2.6	24.2				
Congo, Rep. of	5.9	23.7	7.0	23.6	5.9	14.4	6.2	14.7
Costa Rica	5.2	31.8	7.8	22.2	4.4	20.8	4.6	19.8
Côte d'Ivoire	5.5	19.3	7.3	22.6			5.2	
Croatia							5.3	
Cuba	4.2	18.4	7.2		6.6	12.3		10.9
Cyprus		17.4	3.5	12.9	3.4	11.3		13.2
Czech Republic							5.8	13.6
Denmark	6.9	16.9	6.9	9.5			8.2	13.1
Djibouti						10.5		
Dominican Republic	2.9	15.9	2.2	16.0			1.9	13.2
Ecuador	4.2	23.2	5.6	33.3	3.1	17.2	3.4	15.2
Egypt, Arab Rep. of	4.8	15.8			4.0		4.8	14.9
El Salvador	2.6	27.6	3.9	17.1	2.0	28.1	2.2	
Eritrea								
Estonia							6.9	25.5

TABLE D, *continued*

Country	% of GNP 1970	% of Gov't Spending 1970	% of GNP 1980	% of Gov't Spending 1980	% of GNP 1990	% of Gov't Spending 1990	% of GNP 1995	% of Gov't Spending 1995
Ethiopia		14.1		10.4	3.4	9.4	4.0	13.9
Fiji	4.2	15.6	5.1		4.7			
Finland	5.9		5.3		5.7	11.9	7.6	12.2
France	4.8	24.9	5.0		5.4		6.1	11.1
French Polynesia	0.3							
Gabon	3.2	16.2	2.7				2.8	
Gambia, The	2.3	10.8	3.3		4.2	14.6	6.0	
Georgia								
Germany							4.8	9.5
Ghana	4.3	19.6	3.1	17.1	3.3	24.3		
Greece	1.7	9.6			2.5		2.9	8.2
Guam								
Guatemala	2.0	17.5	1.8	11.9	1.4	11.8	1.7	18.2
Guinea								
Guinea-Bissau								
Guyana	4.7	13.2			4.8	4.4	4.3	8.1
Haiti			1.5	14.9	1.5	20.0		
Honduras	3.1	18.4	3.2	14.2			3.6	16.5
Hong Kong, China	2.4	22.8	2.4	14.6	2.8	17.4	2.9	
Hungary		6.9	4.7	5.2	6.1	7.8	5.3	9.4
Iceland	3.6	17.7	4.4	14.0	5.6		5.0	12.3
India	2.6	10.7	3.0	11.2	3.9	12.2	3.4	11.6
Indonesia	2.6		1.7	8.9	1.0		1.4	7.8
Iran, Islamic Rep. of		9.6	7.5	15.7	4.1	22.4	4.0	17.8
Iraq			3.0					
Ireland	4.8	10.8	6.3		5.6	10.2	6.1	13.5
Israel	5.6	8.1	7.9	7.3	6.2	11.3		
Italy	3.7	11.9			3.2		4.7	9.0
Jamaica	3.6		7.0	13.1	5.4	12.8	6.4	7.7
Japan	3.9	20.4	5.8	19.6				
Jordan	3.7	9.3	6.6	14.4	8.9	17.1	8.7	21.
Kazakhstan					3.2	17.6	4.6	17.6
Kenya	5.0	17.6	6.8	18.1	7.1	17.0	6.8	16.9
Korea, Rep. of	3.4	21.4	3.7	23.7	3.5	22.4	3.7	17.5
Kuwait	4.2	11.2	2.4	8.1	3.5	3.4	5.7	8.9
Kyrgyz Republic				22.2	8.4	22.5	6.9	23.1
Lao PDR				1.3			2.3	
Latvia			3.3	15.3	3.8	10.8	6.7	16.8
Lebanon		16.8		13.2			2.6	8.7
Lesotho	3.0	16.2	5.1	14.8	3.6	12.2		
Liberia	2.0	9.5	5.7	24.3				
Libya	4.5	17.4	3.4					
Lithuania				15.4	4.8	13.8	5.7	21.8
Luxembourg	3.6	14.8	5.7	14.9	2.6	10.4	4.1	15.1
Macao						10.7		
Macedonia, FYR							5.5	18.7
Madagascar			4.4		1.5			
Malawi	4.6	13.2	3.4	8.4	3.3	11.1	5.5	
Malaysia	4.2	17.7	6.0	14.7	5.5	18.3		
Maldives					6.3	10.0	6.4	10.5

TABLE D, *continued*

Country	% of GNP 1970	% of Gov't Spending 1970	% of GNP 1980	% of Gov't Spending 1980	% of GNP 1990	% of Gov't Spending 1990	% of GNP 1995	% of Gov't Spending 1995
Mali			3.7	30.8			2.2	
Malta	6.3	13.0	3.0	7.8	4.0	8.3	5.2	11.4
Mauritania	3.3	21.9					5.1	16.2
Mauritius	3.1	11.5	5.3	11.6	3.5	11.8		
Mexico	2.3		4.7	20.4	3.7	12.8	4.9	23.0
Moldova					5.6	17.2	7.7	22.9
Mongolia		15.6		19.1	12.9	17.6	6.0	17.0
Morocco	3.5	16.6	6.1	18.5	5.5	26.1	5.8	24.7
Mozambique			4.4	12.1	6.0	12.0		
Myanmar	3.1	17.9	1.7					
Namibia					7.4		8.4	24.6
Nepal	0.6	6.7	1.8	10.5	2.0	8.5	3.2	14.0
Netherlands	7.2		7.6	22.6	6.0	14.8	5.2	8.7
New Caledonia	0.2							
New Zealand	4.7		5.8	23.1	6.6			
Nicaragua	2.3	18.1	3.4	10.4			3.7	
Niger	1.1	17.7	3.1	22.9				
Nigeria					1.0		0.9	11.5
Norway	5.4	15.5	6.5	13.7	7.3	14.6	8.1	16.7
Oman			2.1	4.1	3.5	11.1	4.4	16.3
Pakistan	1.7	4.2	2.0	5.0	2.6		2.8	7.1
Panama	5.3	22.1	4.9	19.0	4.9	20.9		
Papua New Guinea	4.5	13.2						
Paraguay	2.2	15.3	1.5	16.4	1.1	9.1	3.4	18.0
Peru	3.3	18.8	3.1	15.2				
Philippines	2.8	24.4	1.7	9.1	2.9	10.1	2.2	
Poland							5.2	
Portugal	1.5	6.6	3.8		4.3		5.5	
Puerto Rico	7.8							
Qatar	3.3	8.9	2.6	7.2	3.4			
Reunion			15.6					
Romania		8.0	3.3	6.7	2.8	7.3		
Russian Federation	3.9		3.5		3.5			
Rwanda	2.3	26.6	2.7	21.6				
Samoa		20.0			4.2	10.7		
Saudi Arabia	3.5	9.8	4.1	8.7	6.0	17.8	5.5	17.7
Senegal	3.8	21.3			4.0	26.9	3.6	33.1
Seychelles	4.2	11.5	5.8	14.4	8.1	14.8	7.6	16.3
Sierra Leone	3.2	17.5	3.5	11.8				
Singapore	3.1	11.7	2.8	7.3	3.0	18.2	3.0	23.4
Slovak Republic					5.1		5.1	
Slovenia							5.8	12.6
Solomon Islands		13.8	5.6	11.2				
Somalia	1.0	7.6	1.0	8.7				
South Africa					6.5		6.8	20.5
Spain	2.0	15.2	2.3	14.7	4.4	9.4	4.9	12.8
Sri Lanka	4.0	13.6	2.7	7.7	2.7	8.1	3.0	8.1
St. Kitts and Nevis		9.7	5.3	9.4	2.8		3.7	9.8
St. Lucia								
St. Vincent and the Grenadines	5.8				6.9	13.8		

TABLE D, *continued*

Country	% of GNP 1970	% of Gov't Spending 1970	% of GNP 1980	% of Gov't Spending 1980	% of GNP 1990	% of Gov't Spending 1990	% of GNP 1995	% of Gov't Spending 1995
Sudan	3.9	12.6	4.8	9.1	0.9	2.8		
Suriname	7.3	17.9	6.7	22.5				
Swaziland	4.9	17.3	6.0		5.9	19.5	7.6	19.9
Sweden	7.6		9.0	14.1	7.7	13.8	8.1	11.6
Switzerland	3.9	18.4	4.9	18.8	4.8	18.7	5.3	14.7
Syrian Arab Republic	3.9	9.4	4.6	8.1	4.3	17.3	3.3	11.2
Tajikistan				29.2	9.7	24.7	2.4	16.1
Tanzania		16.0		11.2	3.4	11.4		
Thailand	3.2	17.3	3.4	20.6	3.6	20.0	4.1	20.1
Togo	2.2	19.0	5.6	19.4	5.6	26.4		
Trinidad and Tobago	3.4	14.0	4.0	11.5	4.0	11.6		
Tunisia	7.1	23.2	5.4	16.4	6.2	13.5	6.8	17.4
Turkey	2.1	13.7	2.2	10.5	2.1		2.2	
Turkmenistan					4.3	21.0		
Uganda	4.1	17.7	1.2	11.3	1.5	11.5	2.6	21.4
Ukraine	5.5	28.1	5.6	24.5	5.2	19.7	7.2	
United Arab Emirates		1.3			1.7	14.6	1.8	16.3
United Kingdom	5.3	14.1	5.6	13.9	4.9		5.4	
United States	7.5	22.7	6.7		5.2	12.3		
Uruguay	3.9	26.1	2.3	10.0	3.1	15.9	2.8	
Uzbekistan				23.0	9.5	20.4	7.4	22.8
Vanuatu		32.1			4.4		4.9	
Venezuela	4.1	22.9	4.4	14.7	3.1	12.0		
Vietnam						7.5		
Yemen, Rep. of								
Yugoslavia, FR (Serb./Mont.)								
Zambia	4.5	9.0	4.5	7.6	2.3	8.7	2.2	7.1
Zimbabwe	3.4		6.6	13.7	10.4			
World	3.1	12.1	3.5	12.2	3.4	13.2	3.4	13.0
Low and middle income	2.4	10.0	3.0	11.6	3.1	13.2	3.3	13.2
Sub-Saharan Africa	3.8	16.0	4.0	15.5	3.4	12.8	3.4	15.2
East Asia and Pacific	1.6	6.3	2.4	9.7	2.3	12.8	2.3	10.7
South Asia	2.5	10.0	2.7	10.2	3.5	11.9	3.3	11.0
Europe and Central Asia	4.0	17.5	3.7	16.2	4.3	17.1	5.0	18.1
Latin America and the Caribbean	3.0	14.5	3.8	17.8	3.0	13.6	4.6	18.1
Middle East and N. Africa	5.0	15.9	6.1	16.2	4.7	21.1	4.9	17.0
High income	5.4	19.3	5.8	17.3	4.9	13.4	5.0	11.4

Source: Columns 1 through 8: UNESCO 1999a; columns 1 and 2 supplemented by UNESCO 1999b.

TABLE E. EXPENDITURES ON TERTIARY EDUCATION

Country	Public Current Spending on Higher Education as % of Total Public Current Spending on Education		Tertiary Expenditure per Student as % of GNP per Capita	
	1985 or closest yr.	1995 or LYA**	1980	1995
Afghanistan				
Albania		10.3		36
Algeria				
Angola				
Argentina	19.2	21.0	10	17
Armenia	13.2		19	
Australia	30.5	29.8	30	30
Austria	16.6	21.4	38	32
Azerbaijan		7.8		13
Bahamas, The				
Bahrain				
Bangladesh	10.4	7.9	47	30
Barbados	22.3			
Belarus	14.0	11.0	33	20
Belgium	16.7	20.3	35	35
Belize	2.3	7.4		
Benin		18.8		240
Bermuda	21.4			
Bolivia		28.7		67
Botswana	17.2		665	
Brazil			0	
Brunei				
Bulgaria	12.4	15.8		21
Burkina Faso	30.7		3,371	
Burundi	19.8	15.6		941
Cambodia				
Cameroon	27.4		363	
Canada	28.7	34.7*	28	36
Central African Republic	18.8	24.0		
Chad		9.0		234
Chile	20.3*	18.1		21
China	21.8	15.4		81
Colombia	21.2	18.5	41	29
Comoros		17.2		
Congo, Dem. Rep. of	28.7		749	
Congo, Rep. of	34.4	28.0		224
Costa Rica	41.4	30.9	76	44
Côte d'Ivoire	17.1	16.4		
Croatia				
Cuba	12.9	15.4	29	
Cyprus	4.2	6.5		
Czech Republic		14.7		41
Denmark	21.9	22.8		55
Djibouti				
Dominican Republic	20.8	9.0		5
Ecuador	17.8	18.1	22	34
Egypt, Arab Rep. of		35.4		108
El Salvador		7.2	103	8
Eritrea				
Estonia		17.6		40

Country	Public Current Spending on Higher Education as % of Total Public Current Spending on Education		Tertiary Expenditure per Student as % of GNP per Capita	
	1985 or closest yr.	1995 or LYA**	1980	1995
Ethiopia	14.4	14.9		592
Fiji				
Finland	18.7	28.8	28	46
France	12.9	17.0	22	24
French Polynesia				
Gabon				
Gambia, The	13.8	10.9		235
Georgia		18.5		28
Germany		22.6		35
Ghana	12.5			
Greece	20.1	22.6*	27	29
Guam				
Guatemala		15.5		33
Guinea	23.5	17.2		498
Guinea-Bissau				
Guyana	17.8	7.7		
Haiti	10.8		65	
Honduras	21.3	16.6	72	59
Hong Kong, China	25.1	37.1		52
Hungary	16.9	18.3	75	73
Iceland		20.8		
India	15.3	13.7		78
Indonesia				
Iran, Islamic Rep. of	10.7	22.9		62
Iraq	25.0*			
Ireland	17.7	22.6	39	38
Israel	18.9	18.2	52	31
Italy	10.2	15.0		23
Jamaica	19.4	23.1	167	193
Japan		12.1	21	16
Jordan	34.1	34.9		111
Kazakhstan		12.5		20
Kenya	12.4	13.7	808	540
Korea, Rep. of	10.9	9.5*	7	6
Kuwait	16.7	29.9	28	
Kyrgyz Republic	8.8	8.3		49
Lao PDR		4.0		55
Latvia	10.3	12.2*		45
Lebanon				
Lesotho	22.3	17.0	642	399
Liberia				
Libya				
Lithuania		18.0		51
Luxembourg	3.3	4.8		
Macao				
Macedonia, FYR		22.2		
Madagascar	27.2			
Malawi	23.3	20.5	1,137	979
Malaysia	14.6	16.8	149	77
Maldives				

Country	Public Current Spending on Higher Education as % of Total Public Current Spending on Education		Tertiary Expenditure per Student as % of GNP per Capita	
	1985 or closest yr.	1995 or LYA**	1980	1995
Mali	13.4	17.7		522
Malta	8.2	12.7		
Mauritania	17.5	20.1		157
Mauritius			163	
Mexico		17.2		61
Moldova				
Mongolia	17.3	17.9		74
Morocco	17.1	16.5		74
Mozambique				
Myanmar		11.7		21
Namibia		9.4		86
Nepal	33.4	17.3	272	156
Netherlands	26.4	29.9	54	44
New Caledonia				
New Zealand	28.3	29.4	33	39
Nicaragua	23.2		86	
Niger			1,493	
Nigeria			345	
Norway	13.5	27.1	29	50
Oman	15.3	5.8		
Pakistan	18.2	13.2	236	
Panama	20.4	24.8	29	47
Papua New Guinea				
Paraguay	23.8	19.7		52
Peru			5	
Philippines	22.5			
Poland	18.2	14.6*		42
Portugal	12.7	16.4		25
Puerto Rico				
Qatar				
Reunion				
Romania		15.9*		40
Russian Federation				
Rwanda	11.5			
Samoa				
Saudi Arabia	27.1	17.8		63
Senegal	19.0	23.2		
Seychelles				
Sierra Leone	15.1			
Singapore	27.9	34.8	31	32
Slovak Republic		16.7		39
Slovenia		16.9		38
Solomon Islands				
Somalia				
South Africa	24.8	15.4		59
Spain		15.1		18
Sri Lanka	9.8	12.2	62	64
St. Kitts and Nevis	2.1	11.6		
St. Lucia	4.5	12.5		
St. Vincent and the Grenadines				

TABLE E, *continued*

Country	Public Current Spending on Higher Education as % of Total Public Current Spending on Education		Tertiary Expenditure per Student as % of GNP per Capita	
	1985 or closest yr.	1995 or LYA**	1980	1995
Sudan			441	
Suriname	7.7	7.6		
Swaziland	21.0	27.5		
Sweden	13.1	27.7*	26	76
Switzerland	18.1	19.7	56	
Syrian Arab Republic	33.6*	25.9*		
Tajikistan	7.7	10.3	30	39
Tanzania	12.7		2,195	
Thailand	13.2	19.4		25
Togo	22.8	32.9	892	521
Trinidad and Tobago	8.9	13.3	55	77
Tunisia	18.2	18.8	194	89
Turkey	23.9	34.7	108	51
Turkmenistan				
Uganda	13.2			
Ukraine	13.5	10.7	39	20
United Arab Emirates				
United Kingdom	19.8	23.7*	80	44
United States	25.1	25.2*	48	23
Uruguay	22.4	27.0		28
Uzbekistan		9.7		28
Vanuatu		6.4		
Venezuela			57	
Vietnam				
Yemen, Rep. of				
Yugoslavia, FR (Serb./Mont.)		21.8		
Zambia	18.3	23.2	762	160
Zimbabwe	9.0	17.3*	260	234
World	18.8	16.0	163	77
Low and middle income	18.5	15.7	259	91
Sub-Saharan Africa	19.1	16.7	802	422
East Asia and Pacific	21.4	15.4	149	76
South Asia	15.3	13.1	143	74
Europe and Central Asia	17.3	18.3	67	36
Latin America and the Caribbean	19.5	18.1	19	43
Middle East and N. Africa	15.9	25.5	194	82
High income	20.3	18.2	39	26

*Data include capital expenditures. These data are not included in regional and world aggregations.
**LYA Last year available.
Source: Columns 1 and 2: UNESCO 1998a; columns 3 and 4: World Bank 1998.

TABLE F. OTHER EDUCATIONAL DATA

Country	Summary Publication and Citation Statistics on Research in the Sciences and Social Sciences				Nationals Studying Abroad as % of Students at Home	Tertiary Science Enrollment as % of Total Tertiary	
	Number of Papers	Number of Papers	Number of Citations	Number of Citations			
	1981	1995	1981–85	1993–97	1995 or LYA**	1987–88	1995
Afghanistan						22	
Albania						35	24
Algeria	103	291	561	1,814	7.4	14	52
Angola						26	
Argentina	1,051	2,589	10,015	28,240		37	30
Armenia		248		1,249			
Australia	10,519	18,088	147,733	301,320		32	29
Austria	2,735	5,287	28,921	94,144	4.1	34	29
Azerbaijan		208		444			38
Bahamas, The							
Bahrain							39
Bangladesh	123	355	1,385	2,299		34	
Barbados						39	19
Belarus		1,033		4,220	2.2		35
Belgium	4,273	8,167	67,888	166,223		15	25
Belize							
Benin						18	19
Bermuda							
Bolivia						21	
Botswana						26	24
Brazil	1,913	5,440	14,446	55,170	0.7	40	22
Brunei							6
Bulgaria	1,109	1,374	4,683	11,198		48	25
Burkina Faso						21	18
Burundi						45	
Cambodia							
Cameroon	38	144	149	1,386	18.2	35	
Canada	19,560	33,426	299,529	669,313	1.4	22	
Central African Republic						34	
Chad						12	14
Chile	673	1,376	6,521	15,940		17	42
China	1,293	11,435	8,517	77,841	2.1	18	37
Colombia	135	294	1,015	4,138		36	31
Comoros							
Congo, Dem. Rep. of						34	
Congo, Rep. of						8	11
Costa Rica	71	193	538	1,882		41	18
Côte d'Ivoire	163	98	520	1,515		28	26
Croatia		898		8,138			38
Cuba	139	344	382	2,289		25	23
Cyprus					104.1	33	19
Czech Republic		3,150		21,106			36
Denmark	3,855	6,414	73,093	147,212		38	24
Djibouti							
Dominican Republic							
Ecuador						21	
Egypt, Arab Rep. of	1,304	2,091	5,133	9,730	0.9	38	15
El Salvador						50	25
Eritrea							
Estonia		390		4,314			34

TABLE F, *continued*

Country	Summary Publication and Citation Statistics on Research in the Sciences and Social Sciences				Nationals Studying Abroad as % of Students at Home	Tertiary Science Enrollment as % of Total Tertiary	
	Number of Papers	Number of Papers	Number of Citations	Number of Citations			
	1981	1995	1981–85	1993–97	1995 or LYA**	1987–88	1995
Ethiopia	47	193	521	1,609		37	36
Fiji						35	
Finland	2,615	5,732	41,094	119,304		50	37
France	23,101	41,039	319,296	782,069	1.5		24
French Polynesia							
Gabon						22	
Gambia, The							
Georgia							48
Germany	33,602	53,160	467,933	1,068,338	2.1	46	35
Ghana	81	116	435	892		30	
Greece	968	3,259	8,981	34,790	13.3	43	30
Guam							
Guatemala						39	
Guinea							
Guinea-Bissau							
Guyana						41	43
Haiti							
Honduras						29	26
Hong Kong, China	375	2,382	3,770	24,706	36.1	43	36
Hungary	2,598	3,047	21,591	39,407		32	29
Iceland	44	255	852	5,521			
India	13,623	14,883	56,464	90,162	0.7	32	
Indonesia	89	310	694	3,364	1.0	39	28
Iran, Islamic Rep. of	253	438	894	2,441	2.6	39	37
Iraq	208	84	774	327		33	
Ireland	881	1,891	9,047	27,772	9.1	35	31
Israel	4,934	8,279	73,973	148,182	4.8	13	27
Italy	9,618	24,695	133,715	442,636	2.1	39	28
Jamaica	136	154	1,143	1,261		37	
Japan	27,177	58,910	378,092	930,981	1.6	26	23
Jordan	56	278	263	1,018	15.4		28
Kazakhstan		221		690	3.4		42
Kenya	362	542	2,963	6,364		21	
Korea, Rep. of	234	5,393	2,656	43,561	3.1	31	39
Kuwait	134	324	695	1,576		35	23
Kyrgyz Republic							28
Lao PDR						42	45
Latvia		275		2,234			34
Lebanon	111	110	572	715	12.9	45	17
Lesotho						16	25
Liberia							
Libya							
Lithuania		292		3,218			
Luxembourg							
Macao							
Macedonia, FYR							41
Madagascar						20	23
Malawi						37	18
Malaysia	229	587	1,332	3,450	21.5	34	
Maldives							

Country	Summary Publication and Citation Statistics on Research in the Sciences and Social Sciences				Nationals Studying Abroad as % of Students at Home	Tertiary Science Enrollment as % of Total Tertiary	
	Number of Papers	Number of Papers	Number of Citations	Number of Citations			
	1981	1995	1981–85	1993–97	1995 or LYA**	1987–88	1995
Mali						3	
Malta						38	13
Mauritania						12	8
Mauritius							
Mexico	907	2,901	8,779	28,589	0.8	36	33
Moldova					8.0		34
Mongolia						56	24
Morocco	92	554	597	3,031	11.9	59	29
Mozambique						25	50
Myanmar						32	36
Namibia						9	5
Nepal						30	17
Netherlands	7,270	16,702	143,320	384,977	2.3	30	20
New Caledonia							
New Zealand	2,200	3,539	23,181	53,775		29	20
Nicaragua						43	
Niger						24	
Nigeria	1,062	741	3,670	3,559		30	41
Norway	2,306	4,264	34,601	70,109	4.7	30	19
Oman						34	
Pakistan	189	618	935	2,803	2.4		
Panama	32	80	525	1,818		32	26
Papua New Guinea	114	105	584	989		11	
Paraguay						50	25
Peru	72	143	620	1,614	1.1	25	
Philippines	243	294	1,379	2,893			31
Poland	4,563	7,097	30,960	71,003	1.4	37	29
Portugal	237	1,580	2,956	19,617	2.7	35	30
Puerto Rico							
Qatar						10	
Reunion							
Romania	950	1,154	3,970	7,894	2.0		51
Russian Federation		24,958		159,065	0.3		49
Rwanda						25	
Samoa							14
Saudi Arabia	299	1,409	1,494	7,826	2.8	34	
Senegal						31	
Seychelles							45
Sierra Leone							30
Singapore	192	1,914	1,302	16,257	19.7	29	
Slovak Republic		1,901		8,691			
Slovenia		693		7,969			18
Solomon Islands							29
Somalia						18	
South Africa	2,211	3,413	19,549	35,056		47	57
Spain	3,462	15,367	31,272	227,637	1.3	32	
Sri Lanka	121	139	616	967		37	
St. Kitts and Nevis						14	
St. Lucia						40	
St. Vincent and the Grenadines							

TABLE F, *continued*

Country	Summary Publication and Citation Statistics on Research in the Sciences and Social Sciences				Nationals Studying Abroad as % of Students at Home	Tertiary Science Enrollment as % of Total Tertiary	
	Number of Papers	Number of Papers	Number of Citations	Number of Citations			
	1981	1995	1981–85	1993–97	1995 or LYA**	1987–88	1995
Sudan	133	101	615	852		27	
Suriname							
Swaziland							22
Sweden	6,891	12,825	145,644	289,268	3.5	42	29
Switzerland	6,160	11,510	146,664	341,129	5.2	40	32
Syrian Arab Republic					6.8	31	29
Tajikistan							23
Tanzania	98	198	554	2,638		9	39
Thailand	373	648	2,419	8,398	1.3	25	19
Togo						52	16
Trinidad and Tobago	57	82	269	557		43	45
Tunisia	111	300	567	2,148	9.4	31	24
Turkey	332	2,449	2,139	15,404	3.2		21
Turkmenistan							
Uganda						41	13
Ukraine		3,723		16,679	1.4		
United Arab Emirates	11	224	30	1,352		46	
United Kingdom	38,580	61,734	684,437	1,334,782	1.3	42	31
United States	174,123	249,386	3,496,945	6,475,200	0.2		
Uruguay	42	170	588	2,763		48	
Uzbekistan		356		1,371			
Vanuatu							
Venezuela	348	660	3,962	7,847		26	
Vietnam	49	192	203	1,657			
Yemen, Rep. of						12	
Yugoslavia, FR (Serb./Mont.)	1,148	747	8,150	5,618	4.5		
Zambia	46	81	242	552			
Zimbabwe	96	212	522	1,687		32	23
World	459,457	772,036	7,138,219	15,116,724		29	33
Low and middle income	72,871	108,929	365,818	830,881		28	34
Sub-Saharan Africa	4,337	5,839	29,740	56,110		29	36
East Asia and Pacific	2,390	13,571	15,128	98,592		22	35
South Asia	14,056	15,995	59,400	96,231		32	17
Europe and Central Asia	43,975	53,543	201,892	398,790		38	39
Latin America and the Caribbean	5,576	14,426	48,803	152,108		35	27
Middle East and N. Africa	2,537	5,555	10,855	29,050		35	30
High income	386,586	663,107	6,772,401	14,285,843		34	29

**LYA Last year available.
Source: Columns 1 through 4: ISI 1998; column 5: UNESCO 1998a; column 6: UNDP 1992; column 7: UNDP 1998.
Data for column 5 are not aggregated by region because only 50 countries are represented.

TABLE G. OTHER DATA

Country	Adult Literacy Rate (%) 1970	Adult Literacy Rate (%) 1995	GDP per Capita 1965	GDP per Capita 1995	Life Expectancy at Birth (Years) 1995	Human Development Index (HDI) 1995
Afghanistan						
Albania		85			70.6	0.656
Algeria	25	62	1,584	2,569	68.1	0.746
Angola		42	1,062	710	47.4	0.344
Argentina	93	96	5,018	5,634	72.6	0.888
Armenia		99			70.9	0.674
Australia		99	8,823	15,952	78.2	0.932
Austria		99	6,144	13,334	76.7	0.933
Azerbaijan		96			71.1	0.623
Bahamas, The	95	98		10,687	73.2	0.893
Bahrain	53	85		9,302	72.2	0.872
Bangladesh	25	38	1,136	1,662	56.9	0.371
Barbados	92	97	3,274	6,755	76.0	0.909
Belarus		98			69.3	0.783
Belgium	99	99	6,749	13,778	76.9	0.933
Belize		70		4,265	74.2	0.807
Benin	10	37	1,191	1,082	54.4	0.378
Bermuda						
Bolivia	58	83	1,346	1,845	60.5	0.593
Botswana	44	70	574	2,398	51.7	0.678
Brazil	68	83	1,871	4,114	66.6	0.809
Brunei	57	88			75.1	0.889
Bulgaria	94	98		5,461	71.2	0.789
Burkina Faso	8	19	373	490	46.3	0.219
Burundi	18	35	390	426	44.5	0.241
Cambodia		65			52.9	0.422
Cameroon	32	63	673	912	55.3	0.481
Canada		99	8,664	17,213	79.1	0.960
Central African Republic	13	60	663	516	48.4	0.347
Chad	24	48	736	357	47.2	0.318
Chile	88	95	3,264	5,703	75.1	0.893
China	52	82	577	2,047	69.2	0.650
Colombia	81	91	1,816	3,774	70.3	0.850
Comoros	42	57	646	480	56.5	0.411
Congo, Dem. Rep. of	44	77	548	211	52.4	0.383
Congo, Rep. of		75	1,084	1,863	51.2	0.519
Costa Rica	88	95	2,459	3,817	76.6	0.889
Côte d'Ivoire	16	40	1,400	1,111	51.8	0.368
Croatia		98			71.6	0.759
Cuba	82	96			75.7	0.729
Cyprus		94	2,717		77.2	0.913
Czech Republic		99			72.4	0.884
Denmark		99	8,436	15,170	75.3	0.928
Djibouti	23	46			49.2	0.324
Dominican Republic	68	82	1,271	2,396	70.3	0.720
Ecuador	75	90	1,591	2,865	69.5	0.767
Egypt, Arab Rep. of	32	51	1,024	1,974	64.8	0.612
El Salvador	56	72	1,739	2,090	69.4	0.604
Eritrea		25			50.2	0.275
Estonia		99			69.2	0.758

TABLE G, *continued*

Country	Adult Literacy Rate (%) 1970	Adult Literacy Rate (%) 1995	GDP per Capita 1965	GDP per Capita 1995	Life Expectancy at Birth (Years) 1995	Human Development Index (HDI) 1995
Ethiopia	16	36	290	321	48.7	0.252
Fiji	74	92	2,160	4,166	72.1	0.869
Finland		99	6,514	12,762	76.4	0.942
France	99	99	7,304	14,286	78.7	0.946
French Polynesia						
Gabon	26	63	2,587	3,718	54.5	0.568
Gambia, The	17	39	724	728	46.0	0.291
Georgia		99			73.2	0.633
Germany		99	7,912	15,419	76.4	0.925
Ghana	31	65	883	1,001	57.0	0.473
Greece	93	97	3,067	7,112	77.9	0.924
Guam						
Guatemala	44	65	1,781	2,147	66.1	0.615
Guinea	16	36	545	778	45.5	0.277
Guinea-Bissau	30	55	612	665	43.4	0.295
Guyana	91	98	1,575	1,417	63.5	0.670
Haiti	24	45	894	525	54.6	0.340
Honduras	54	73	1,121	1,385	68.8	0.573
Hong Kong, China	79	92	3,492	18,240	79.0	0.909
Hungary	98	99		4,874	68.9	0.857
Iceland		99	6,215	13,019	79.2	0.942
India	34	52	751	1,467	61.6	0.451
Indonesia	56	84	608	2,478	64.0	0.679
Iran, Islamic Rep. of	35	69	3,364	3,618	68.5	0.758
Iraq	30	58	4,412		58.5	0.538
Ireland		99	4,000	11,690	76.4	0.930
Israel	93	95	4,644	11,006	77.5	0.913
Italy	95	98	5,691	13,174	78.0	0.922
Jamaica	70	85	2,104	2,473	74.1	0.735
Japan	99	99	4,491	15,338	79.9	0.940
Jordan	54	87	1,604	3,187	68.9	0.729
Kazakhstan		99			67.5	0.695
Kenya	43	78	614	901	53.8	0.463
Korea, Rep. of	87	98	1,058	9,250	71.7	0.894
Kuwait	57	79		8,046	75.4	0.848
Kyrgyz Republic		97			67.9	0.633
Lao PDR	32	57		1,652	52.2	0.465
Latvia		99			68.0	0.704
Lebanon	80	92			69.3	0.796
Lesotho	47	71	409	1,138	58.1	0.469
Liberia			824			
Libya		76			64.3	0.806
Lithuania		99			70.2	0.750
Luxembourg		99	8,569	18,939	76.1	0.900
Macao						
Macedonia, FYR		94			71.9	0.749
Madagascar		46	1,111	586	57.6	0.348
Malawi	38	56	412	501	41.0	0.334
Malaysia	57	84	1,671	6,916	71.4	0.834
Maldives	87	93			63.3	0.683

Country	Adult Literacy Rate (%)		GDP per Capita	GDP per Capita	Life Expectancy at Birth (Years)	Human Development Index (HDI)
	1970	1995	1965	1995	1995	1995
Mali	7	31	435	523	47.0	0.236
Malta		91	1,487	8,523	76.5	0.899
Mauritania	27	38	882	895	52.5	0.361
Mauritius	65	83	3,136	6,821	70.9	0.833
Mexico	75	90	3,351	5,899	72.1	0.855
Moldova		99			67.8	0.610
Mongolia	63	83		1,420	64.8	0.669
Morocco	21	44	1,221	2,109	65.7	0.557
Mozambique	16	40	1,265	783	46.3	0.281
Myanmar	72	83	415		58.9	0.481
Namibia		76	2,325	2,834	55.8	0.644
Nepal	14	28	650	1,177	55.9	0.351
Netherlands		99	7,396	13,917	77.5	0.941
New Caledonia						
New Zealand		99	9,032	12,582	76.6	0.939
Nicaragua	57	66	2,246	1,436	67.5	0.547
Niger	6	14	641	428	47.5	0.207
Nigeria	21	57	624	951	51.4	0.391
Norway		99	6,950	17,171	77.6	0.943
Oman		59		7,862	70.3	0.771
Pakistan	20	38	889	1,461	62.8	0.453
Panama	79	91	2,014	3,481	73.4	0.868
Papua New Guinea	47	72	1,700	1,799	56.8	0.507
Paraguay	81	92	1,277	2,122	69.1	0.707
Peru	71	89	2,501	2,531	67.7	0.729
Philippines	84	95	1,243	1,760	67.4	0.677
Poland	98	99		4,396	71.1	0.851
Portugal	78	90	2,407	8,075	74.8	0.892
Puerto Rico			4,414			
Qatar	58	79		11,473	71.1	0.840
Reunion			1,526			
Romania	96	98	590	1,725	69.6	0.767
Russian Federation		99			65.5	0.769
Rwanda			350	412		
Samoa		98			68.4	0.694
Saudi Arabia	36	63	5,991	6,510	70.7	0.778
Senegal	15	33	1,143	1,116	50.3	0.342
Seychelles		88	1,338		72.0	0.845
Sierra Leone	13	31	1,114	609	34.7	0.185
Singapore	74	91	1,864	15,774	77.1	0.896
Slovak Republic		99			70.9	0.875
Slovenia		96			73.2	0.887
Solomon Islands		62		2,219	71.1	0.560
Somalia			959			
South Africa	70	82	2,617	3,150	64.1	0.717
Spain	93	97	4,580	10,132	77.7	0.935
Sri Lanka	80	90	1,179	2,495	72.5	0.716
St. Kitts and Nevis		90		5,407	69.0	0.854
St. Lucia		82		3,797	71.0	0.839
St. Vincent and the Grenadines		82		3,802	72.0	0.845

TABLE G, *continued*

Country	Adult Literacy Rate (%)		GDP per Capita	GDP per Capita	Life Expectancy at Birth (Years)	Human Development Index (HDI)
	1970	1995	1965	1995	1995	1995
Sudan	21	46			52.2	0.343
Suriname	82	93	2,272		70.9	0.796
Swaziland	49	77	1,705	2,603	58.8	0.597
Sweden		99	9,402	14,393	78.4	0.936
Switzerland		99	11,150	15,667	78.2	0.930
Syrian Arab Republic	41	71	2,011	4,977	68.1	0.749
Tajikistan		99			66.9	0.575
Tanzania	37	68	371		50.6	0.358
Thailand	78	94	1,136	4,869	69.5	0.838
Togo	23	52	489	464	50.5	0.380
Trinidad and Tobago	92	98	6,428	8,277	73.1	0.880
Tunisia	28	67	1,236	3,158	68.7	0.744
Turkey	57	82	1,812	3,935	68.5	0.782
Turkmenistan		98			64.9	0.660
Uganda	37	62	614	627	40.5	0.340
Ukraine		98			68.5	0.665
United Arab Emirates	54	79		13,855	74.4	0.855
United Kingdom		99	7,679	13,711	76.8	0.932
United States		99	11,649	18,980	76.4	0.943
Uruguay	93	97	3,698	5,401	72.7	0.885
Uzbekistan		99			67.5	0.659
Vanuatu		64		1,513	66.3	0.559
Venezuela	76	91	7,512	6,678	72.3	0.860
Vietnam	73	94			66.4	0.560
Yemen, Rep. of		38			56.7	0.356
Yugoslavia, FR (Serb./Mont.)			2,407			
Zambia	48	78	1,110	578	42.7	0.378
Zimbabwe	66	85	946	1,161	48.9	0.507
World	53	76	2,641	4,532	66.3	0.647
Low and middle income	48	71	1,031	2,208	64.3	0.593
Sub-Saharan Africa	30	56	841	933	51.2	0.385
East Asia and Pacific	55	83	632	2,253	68.0	0.654
South Asia	32	49	805	1,495	61.3	0.446
Europe and Central Asia	84	96	1,500	3,864	68.0	0.751
Latin America anf the Caribbean	73	86	2,738	4,348	69.3	0.801
Middle East and N. Africa	32	60	2,201	3,228	66.1	0.669
High income	95	98	7,665	15,358	77.2	0.934

Source: Columns 1 and 2: UNDP 1998; Columns 3 and 4: Gallup 1999; columns 5 and 6: UNDP 1998.

II: Selected Definitions

Attainment rates

These rates measure the highest level of education in which individuals were enrolled. The data reflect the attainment rates for the population that is over age 25. Attainment rates do not imply that all students completed this level of education.

Citation statistics over 5-year time periods

The Institute for Scientific Information (ISI) database is used to track publication and citation statistics, and typically attributes citations to the year the paper was published. Recent years therefore show dramatically lower citation numbers than earlier years, as there has been less time for newer papers to be cited.

To track trends in citations over time, ISI developed a 5-year-window approach. Each 5-year block measures citations made in a time period for only those papers published in that period. More recent 5-year windows are therefore comparable to older time periods, and growth or decline in citation numbers over time can be noted.

GDP per capita

Real GDP per capita is expressed in constant dollars using the Chain index (1985 international prices). For years up to the early 1990s, data are supplied directly from the *Penn World Tables 5.6*. In cases where the *Penn World Tables* do not have data for a more recent year, the World Bank's figures for GDP per capita are consulted. Because the World Bank figures are expressed in 1987 international dollars, the rate of change of GDP per capita from year to year is extracted from the World Bank data and applied to the *Penn World Table* base. The resulting figure is expressed in 1985 dollars. Data are courtesy of John Gallup, Center for International Development, Harvard University.

Gross enrollment ratio

The gross enrollment ratio is the total enrollment at a given educational level, regardless of age, divided by the population of the age group that typically corresponds to that level of education. The specification of age groups varies by country, based on different national systems of education and the duration of schooling at the first and second levels. For tertiary education, the ratio is expressed as a percentage of the population in the 5-year age group following the official secondary school-leaving age. Gross enrollment ratios may exceed 100 percent if individuals outside the age cohort corresponding to a particular educational level are enrolled in that level.

Human Development Index (HDI)

This index measures the average achievements in a country in three basic dimensions of human development—longevity, knowledge, and a decent standard of living. A composite index, the HDI, thus contains three variables: life expectancy, educational attainment (adult literacy and combined primary, secondary, and tertiary enrollment), and real GDP per capita (in dollars adjusted for purchasing-power parity). The HDI is calculated by the United Nations Development Programme.

Life expectancy at birth

This is the number of years a newborn infant would live if prevailing patterns of mortality at the time of birth were to stay the same throughout the child's life.

Public current spending on higher education as percentage of total public current spending on education

This measures the percentage of public spending on education that is devoted to tertiary education. Only current spending (i.e., recurring, noncapital expenses) is considered.

Public expenditure on education as percentage of GNP

This measures the total public expenditure on education (both current and capital expenses) expressed as a percentage of the gross national product (GNP) for a given year. This indicator shows the proportion of a country's wealth generated during a given year that has been devoted by government authorities to the development of education.

Public expenditure on education as percentage of government expenditure

This measures the total public expenditure on education (both current and capital expenses) expressed as a percentage of total government expenditure in a given year. This indicator shows the proportion of a government's total expenditure for a given year that has been spent on education.

Tertiary education

Education at the tertiary level (International Standard Classification of Education, ISCED, levels five, six, and seven), includes universities, teachers' colleges, and higher professional schools—requiring as a minimum condition of admission the successful completion of education at the secondary level, or evidence of the attainment of an equivalent level of knowledge.

III: Primary Data Sources

Barro, Robert, and Jong-Wha Lee. 1993. "International Comparisons of Educational Attainment." NBER Working Paper 4349.

———. 1994. *Data Set for a Panel of 138 Countries.* Harvard University, Cambridge, Mass., January. Mimeo.

———. 1996. "International Measures of Schooling Years and Schooling Quality." *American Economic Review* 86(2): 218–23.

Bloom, David, and Francisco Rivera-Batiz. 1999. *Global Trends in the Financing of Higher Education: Prospects and Challenges for the Next Decade,* Statistical Appendix. Unpublished.

Drèze, Jean, and Amartya K. Sen. 1995. *India: Economic Development and Social Opportunity.* New York: Oxford University Press.

Gallup, John. 1999. Data set expressing GDP per capita in constant dollars using 1985 international prices. Primary data sources are *Penn World Tables 5.6,* Univerisity of Pennsylvania, and *World Development Indicators 1998,* World Bank. Center for International Development, Harvard University, Cambridge, Mass.

ISI (Institute for Scientific Information). 1998. *National Science Indicators on Diskette,* 1981–97, Version 1.5. Philadelphia, Penn: ISI.

Puryear, Jeffrey M., 1992. "International Education Statistics and Research: Status and Problems." *International Journal of Educational Development,* 15(1):79–91, 1995.

Sen, Amartya K. 1989. *Hunger and Public Action.* Oxford, U.K.: Clarendon Press.

UNDP (United Nations Development Programme). 1992. *Human Development Report 1992.* New York: Oxford University Press.

——— . 1998. *Human Development Report 1998.* New York: Oxford University Press.

UNESCO (United Nations Educational, Scientific and Cultural Organization). 1993. *World Education Report 1993.* Paris.

——— . 1998a. *World Statistical Outlook on Higher Education: 1980–1995.* Working document of the World Conference on Higher Education, Paris, October 1998. Paris.

——— .1998b. *UNESCO Statistical Yearbook 1998.* Paris.

————. 1999a. *Division of Statistics Data.* Available at http://unescostat.unesco.org/Index.asp. March, April, May.

————. 1999b. Correspondence about public expenditures on education. Division of Statistics, Paris. Received April.

United Nations Population Division. 1996. *World Population Prospects 1950– 2050.* New York: United Nations.

World Bank 1994. *Higher Education: The Lessons of Experience.* Washington, D.C.

————. 1998. *World Development Indicators 1998.* CD-ROM. Washington, D.C.

————. 1999. *World Development Report 1998/99: Knowledge for Development.* New York: Oxford University Press.